Transform yc

CW00687931

VISION

7 Powerful and Effective Steps to Achieve Results

Clare M Smale

Transform Your Goals with VISION

First published in the United Kingdom in 2013 by Clare M Smale

Copyright © 2013 Clare M Smale

ISBN 978-0-9576983-0-7

A catalogue record for this book is available from the British Library.

Designed by Angela Jones

Printed and bound by CPI Group (UK) Ltd, Croydon, CR0 4YY

Contents

17 PRACTICAL TOOLS...

1 PART ONE

'Ordinary people believe only in the possible. Extraordinary people visualise not what is possible or probable, but rather what is impossible. And by visualising the impossible, they begin to see it as possible.'

Cherie Carter-Scott

Acknowledgements

Transform your goals with VISION is an accumulation of my experiences over the last twenty four years. As a new young teacher in 1989, I had no idea of the direction that my life would take, from teaching in several schools to running my own business as a trainer and coach. There have been times in my life when I have drifted into opportunities. Sometimes I had a clear goal. Both approaches have worked for me, although my biggest achievements have been where I have had a clear vision of what I wanted to achieve, which includes writing this book.

I wish to thank everyone who has contributed directly or indirectly to this book. You know who you are! Particular thanks go to Lisa Barton, Angela Jones, Rachel Gardiner, Sue Green, Helen Hardman, Caroline Talbott, Steve Thom and Sally Walsh. A special thank you goes to Barrie Smale, Will Thomas and Julie Starr for their long term support, coaching and feedback.

Thank you also to the group of people who road tested the activities in this book to get them just right for you. Photos of their work appear throughout the book so I've changed their names to respect confidentiality.

And finally, thank you to the visionaries who generously gave their time to be interviewed so I could discover their magic and write this book for you – they are truly inspirational people.

I would like to dedicate this book to Alice and Emma.

'What is now proved was once impossible.'

William Blake

For more details on how Clare and

inspired2learn can help you achieve success

go to www.inspired2learn.co.uk

Vision

PART ONE
- Why?
- What?
- How?
- Introduction
- Goals & vision

PART TWO — Vision
- Values
- Identity
- Stories
- Images
- Options
- Next steps *
- Activities and things to do – step by step *

PART THREE — Supec – Vision / Peripheral Vision
- What next?

VISION

Introduction

Welcome to VISION

This book is about transforming your goals.

This book will give you a powerful vision of what you want - at home, work or any other area of your life. You will discover what works and use 17 tools to support and help you achieve your dreams and ambitions. Increase your effectiveness, achieve your goals and make things happen. Take away and use a 7 step system with practical activities. The beauty of the VISION system is that the activities and tools can be used time and time again for different situations. You are provided with step by step instructions, plus templates that you can use as many times as you like.

Why should you read VISION?

- You will gain a new perspective on your goals, ambitions and dreams. You will be able to state your goals in a way that is simple, clear, robust and powerful.

- You will work with your goals to develop a vision for the future you want.

- You will gain over 17 practical tools that you can apply in lots of different areas of your life. Develop your skills immediately so that you can achieve the results you want or need.

- All the activities are suitable for complete beginners and if you are a seasoned pro, you will be able to adapt them as much as you like.

- You can apply the VISION system in any area of your life (at home, at work or in relation to your hobbies and interests), no matter what your situation.

- You can learn at your own rate and in the way that suits you best. Work through the exercises on your own or with other people – the choice is yours.

- You will learn a new and unique system, with practical tools to add to your tool kit.

How to use this book

This book is divided into three parts:

Part 1 will show you how this book will help you and then you will prepare your goals using a range of techniques. Part 1 of this book will help you to check that your goals are clear. Then you will be ready to start the VISION system in Part 2.

Part 2 gives you the VISION system in detail. This section contains a range of tools in 7 easy 'how to' steps. Each step is taking you closer to creating your vision.

Part 3 will bring everything you have learnt together and give you some practical ways to assess your progress. Chapters 11 to 13 will help you to decide what you want (or need) to do next.

How to get the most out of this book

1. Skim through for about 15 minutes, reading just the chapter headings. You might also notice sub-headings, bullet points, photos and diagrams. This will give you a sense of the overall structure and the main themes and activities.

2. I recommend that you work through the book in order, a chapter at a time. The book will flow smoothly for you as each chapter builds upon the skills and thinking from the previous one. **The most powerful results will come from working through the activities in the sequence they are presented.** Once you have completed the VISION system for the first time, you can return to different chapters in any order that you like.

3. The approaches have been explained simply to make the book easily accessible, irrespective of your prior level of experience in working with goals. References and signposts for further reading are provided at the end of the book. If you are interested in scientific research and more detail about the approaches and theories used, you will know where to find out more.

4. Write your ideas in the spaces provided. Writing, as well as thinking, will reinforce your thoughts and will enable you to return to (and build upon) your ideas whenever you like. Keep a notebook or spare paper to hand so that you can capture all your insights.

5. Throughout this book there are real case studies and examples to inspire and guide you. I would love to receive your stories too, so that VISION becomes a resource that builds for other people like you.

6. You will have ownership over your thinking and learning as you use this book. There are no right or wrong answers to the activities in each chapter and you will discover fresh ideas and possibilities for yourself. Applying your ideas and what you learn is in your hands.

All the activities in VISION have been tested and modified by people from many different walks of life. Their feedback has enabled me to get them just right for you. When you read this book and follow the 7 steps, you will achieve better results.

This book is about the process of creating your vision. The 7 steps of VISION will show you how to structure your thinking in a particular order to create what you want. The principles in this book work. All you have to do is make them work for you.

The activities in VISION will enable you to consider different aspects of setting and achieving goals. Some of them will support you to change your thinking in relation to achieving what you want and others will help you to develop practical ideas and steps so that you can take action. Remember that you are unique, and some activities will be easier for you than others. Work at your own pace and take as little or as much time as you need to get the best results for you.

VISION is a bit like the bluebell wood on the cover of this book. VISION will help you to see a clearer way forward through the 'stuff' of everyday life – a bit like 'seeing the wood for the trees'. Maybe you can't see the whole situation clearly yet. This could be because you're concentrating on small details or because you're so closely involved. However, there is a path to take you forward.

Imagine being a bird sat on a branch in a tree in a wood. When the bird is asked what it can see, the bird says 'twigs and leaves'.

Now leave the comfort of the branch, spread your wings and circle a little higher over your perch. Start to notice the big tree that you were sat in, with lots of branches and places to sit and preen your feathers or sing. Float higher and circle again and you notice the landscape around you – the fields, hedges, distant houses, streams and much more. You now have endless options for where to roost, feed and nest. At any time you can drop back down into the tree and sit on a branch to rest and be comfortable.

This metaphor, borrowed from Dr David Drake, encourages you to leave your normal perch and consider the bigger picture in relation to your goals. When you are ready, settle down and plan your next steps.

The New Year is typically a time when people set new goals and statistics show (Richard Wiseman 2007) that just 12 % typically achieve their goals a year later. Goals often lack deeper significance and meaning and as a result we are less likely to stick with them. Having vision is the opposite of this.

As you work through this book, VISION will develop goals that you believe in and give you strong reasons for why you will want to achieve them.

VISION will nurture and transform your goals so that you can create a powerful vision of what you want – at home, work or another area of your life.

'When a person becomes crystal clear as to exactly what they want to accomplish, and focuses their time and energy on this one goal, any person can move mountains.'

Jimmy Sweeney

Chapter ONE

The meaning of VISION

'Cherish your visions and your dreams as they are the children of your soul, the blueprints of your ultimate achievements.'

Napoleon Hill

The meaning of VISION

Life isn't perfect and sometimes events or situations get in the way of achieving your goals and dreams. Maybe you have problems that need your attention and other people around you that demand your time. Perhaps you have exciting thoughts and ideas about your future and no clear plan. Time is ticking by and you are caught up in the 'stuff' of day to day life. This might be frustrating you as you know deep down that you are capable of achieving more. As time drifts by your future might seem unclear. The result of this isn't necessarily disastrous. You are probably achieving some good results and being effective a lot of the time. However, are you settling for something that is good and acceptable rather than what you really want?

> 'Good is the enemy of the great. What stops us living our dream isn't a bad thing, it's a good thing.' *Jim Collins*

On the other hand, your goals may be very clear and you could be reading this book right now to give you the extra 'zing' that would be useful – the difference that makes the difference.

Whatever your current thinking regarding your goals, this book will help you.

As a human being operating in a complex world, there are many things that will be out of your direct control and influence. However in achieving your ambitions and the future you want, you can determine your thoughts, focus, attitude and actions.

VISION is a 7 step system that embeds tools and techniques from coaching and Neuro Linguistic Programming (NLP).

Coaching is a way of receiving challenge and support from another person to help you achieve your potential. There is no common definition for coaching and there are many different schools of thought and approaches.

In simple terms, tools and techniques from coaching are designed to help you to focus on your goals and remove obstacles. Best coaching practice is based on the assumption that you have all the answers within you, and this book is just the same. Just like working with a coach, VISION won't tell you what you should do. Instead it will focus on asking you questions about what you want. Questions are used to develop your thinking so that you know for yourself how to achieve your hopes and aspirations.

Neuro Linguistic Programming (NLP) is the study of effective communication, thinking and behaviour. NLP provides tools and techniques that have evolved from finding out what effective people do and how they think. Many coaches use NLP tools and methods extensively in their work and VISION draws upon some of these.

Effectiveness and excellence can be broken down into steps and its component parts taught to others. At the core of this is 'modelling'. In NLP terms, modelling is a process to finding out how a person (or group of people) achieve excellence. This 'excellence' is then broken down into a step by step process so that others can achieve it too. The steps (or model) are then tested in real life to check that they work.

> *'NLP is a modelling of human experience, especially human excellence.'* Michael Hall

Most of us have prior experience of modelling, either because we are parents or because we've had parents. Not many of us have access to parenting courses and although there are a wide range of parenting books and literature, there is no definitive manual. Parenting skills are mostly learnt from modelling either our own parents or other people who have nurtured us through childhood. We copy what we thought was effective and we do our best to avoid what we perceive to be their mistakes. We replicate the best skills and strategies that we see people using to get great results.

Grinder and Bostic St Clair, (2001) define NLP modelling as '…the mapping of tacit knowledge into explicit knowledge'.

There is growing empirical evidence that humans have the ability to learn by imitating the behaviour of others by simulating (or practising) it in their minds. Mirror neurons in your brain enable you to copy others and they were first discovered in monkeys (Gallese et al 1996). Modelling human excellence looks for patterns by asking questions. In the case of this book, I've asked:

- How does having a vision work?

- What are the component parts of a vision?

- What creates a vision?

- When someone has a vision, how do they run the programme in their mind?

- How can that programme be packaged so that it can be copied by other people, and they can run the programme too?

> *'Figure out what you want. Focus on it. Find people who have achieved what you want and find out how they think and act, and then follow their lead.'* Bill Harris

Modelling Visionary People

The unique VISION system presented in this book here is based upon people I have modelled in order to discover their strategy for developing their vision. These case studies were identified as appropriate exemplars of the model of excellence for visionary thinking. In my role as a coach and trainer I have met many people who would love to initiate a radical project in order to improve their experiences and success. They are very often intimidated by the need to conform to accepted opinion, the structures placed upon them and by the scale of the perceived risk involved. There are a few who can overcome such limiting beliefs and it is from these exceptional people that I have chosen my case studies.

The aim of modelling visionary people for this book was to reproduce their formula for success and give it to you. This was done by noting visionary skills, attributes and behaviours that were relevant to all those that were interviewed. Anything that was idiosyncratic to individuals (rather than present in all cases) and therefore not essential to the model, was discarded. Finally, the constituent patterns of the model were coded in to simple steps – the VISION system.

When you have finished working with the VISION system you will be ready to take action. You will be talking about your vision with others, creating excitement and anticipation, putting steps in place and then leading yourself and/or others towards making your vision a reality. VISION is the system and your effectiveness and excellence are the magic.

These 7 steps in this book are the blueprint for what has worked for other successful and effective people – the steps that they all share in common.

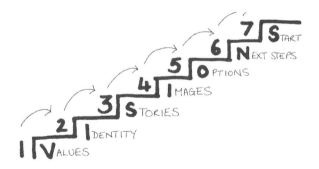

What is the difference between goals and VISION?

A goal is your statement of what you want, commonly defined as an aim, objective or end point.

Your vision then adds imagination, insight and boldness to this. Vision is about looking at the edge - a future or an outcome that you believe in your heart and soul is the right future. You can then focus on making this a reality. Visionaries are inspirational and committed. They know what they want to be, where they want to go and what they want to do.

Before you begin working with the VISION system, it is important to know what you want. Start with the goal in mind.

- What do you hope to become?

- What do you aspire to achieve or reach?

There is considerable debate about the value of setting goals. At one end of the scale we are advised that without goals we cannot expect to achieve what we want; that being aimless will lead to drifting through life, achieving less and being unfulfilled. Others question the value we place (at work or in personal development) on goal setting and argue that happiness isn't dependent upon achieving goals, but instead the quality of our thoughts 'in the moment'. There is an argument that we shouldn't evaluate our happiness or contentment on the basis of what we might achieve in the future (a guess at the best scenario) and that this approach can make unhelpful feelings such as frustration or low self esteem worse.

> *'While setting goals may well help us to achieve goals, they're extremely counter-productive as a pathway towards a happy and fulfilling life.'* Michael Neill, 2013

The concept of vision is helpful in closing the gap between these conflicting arguments about goals. The VISION process will begin by asking you to set goals in the traditional way (chapter two). Next you will consider what is important to you about these goals and why they matter in the world (chapter three). What is their wider purpose to you or others? This means that as well as having an aim or end point, you will also have a sense of doing the right thing for the right reasons.

Vision is a widely used term. If you ask somebody what vision means, they often struggle to give a definition that is clear. The dictionary definition of vision is very helpful in bridging the gap between goals and 'good work' (the right direction for the right reasons). I think it shows how having a vision can give you the best of goal setting methodology, whilst adding the more powerful motivation of fulfilling your purpose in the world.

In this book you will be working with the definitions of vision from the Collins Dictionary (2013):

- **The act, faculty, or manner of perceiving with the eye** – step 4 in the VISION system (chapter five) will show you how to develop and fine tune the pictures, sounds and feelings of what you want.

- **The ability or an instance of great perception, especially of future developments** – all the steps in the VISION system contribute to your ability to perceive the future you want for yourself and your wider 'good work'.

- **A vivid mental image produced by the imagination** – by the time you have completed the VISION system you will have created an even more vivid mental image than you had before, especially through step 4 (chapter five).

- **A person or thing of extraordinary beauty** – Your vision may already be very beautiful to you and if it isn't quite like that for you yet, the VISION system will develop its beauty and magic.

You may also think of this at the level of your 'good work' in the world. By the time you have followed the 7 steps in this book, your personal charisma and inner congruence will be evident. You will communicate what you want to achieve with conviction and passion. Your vision and its potential for 'good work' for others will be held strongly in your mind.

- **The stated aims and objectives of a business or other organisation** – step 6 (chapter 9) in this book will involve creating an action plan. You will put in place actions that will begin to turn your vision into reality. As part of step 6 you will refine your aims (the broad statements of what you want to achieve) and objectives (steps) for doing this. It doesn't matter if your vision is personal, work or business related – the process is the same.

Chapter two will enable you to build a clear picture of your goal(s) and a sense of the future you want. The rest of this book will support you in developing visionary thinking about that future (your goal).

What are the 7 Steps in this book?

VISION – the 7 steps

Step 1   – **V** – Values

Step 2   – **I** – Identity

Step 3   – **S** – Stories

Step 4   – **I** – Images

Step 5   – **O** – Options

Step 6   – **N** – Next steps

Step 7   – **S** – Start

Step 1 - Values

In this first step you will uncover the important thing (or things) about your vision for the future. Knowing this will help you to prioritise your efforts and explain your vision to others in way that is the most powerful it can be. There are several exercises to help you uncover and work with your values.

Step 2 - Identity

Knowing who you are in relation to your vision will be very powerful for you. This may be as simple as taking away a limiting identity such as *'I am a person who lacks confidence'* and replacing it with *'I am a person that can make it happen'*. Some people see identity as the hats they are wearing in different areas of their life and others as their roles or jobs. Our identity is made up of 'I am ...' statements and you will be thinking about which of these are going to be helpful and resourceful in achieving what you want.

Step 3 - Stories

 You are going to need to have compelling evidence that your vision is the right thing to be working towards. You will need proof for yourself and proof that you can give to others. The stories that you tell can provide this proof and I will be giving you the DESERT and PEOPLE story telling systems.

Step 4 - Images

Successful visionaries work with images in their mind of the future they want. These images have particular traits and qualities. In chapter seven I will show you how to create the powerful images, both in your mind's eye for yourself and also in a way that you can describe or show to others.

Step 5 - Options

If you could do anything to make your vision happen, what would it be? This step shares some great creativity techniques to increase the options available to you. The more options you have, the more flexibility you can exhibit when working with others and overcoming challenges.

Step 6 - Next steps

Time for action planning – what specifically are you going to do next? What are the timescales for this? Some people will love your ideas and join you for the fun of the ride, whilst others will want you to be grounded in reality and structure. A balance of both will be healthy for you.

Step 7 - Start

This might sound obvious, although you'd be amazed at how many people fail to take action in the real world. Who are you going to start talking to and what are you going to start doing? Not tomorrow - right now! What will happen if you don't do this?

As with all self help guides and advice, only you can make something new happen. The measure of success in reading this book is whether or not you do something different as a result in real life. Use the 7 step VISION process and take action.

The very first NLP book, 'The Structure of Magic Volume 1', was written by Richard Bandler and John Grinder in 1975. They wrote:

> *'Magic is hidden in the language we speak. The webs that you can tie and untie are at your command if only you pay attention to what you already have (language) and the structure of the incantations for growth.'*

What this means is that words and processes create our reality and you are able to influence or control both of these elements. VISION helps you to build your words and processes so that you can create a future for yourself in your mind that is powerfully and beautifully constructed. You will have the motivation you need to get to work on making the magic happen. You will have the words and structure to enable you to tell others about your vision. Your vision will make sense and you will gain support and involvement from other people.

The vision you hold in your mind will set up a force of attraction. The law of attraction states that your dominant thoughts will bring about results. If your thinking is mostly positive you can expect more positivity to appear in your life and vice versa.

Napoleon Hill and Wallace Wattles were two of the early writers to talk at length about this concept, advocating controlling your thoughts in order to achieve success ('The Law of Success in 16 lessons' (1928), 'Think and Grow Rich' (1937) and the 'Science of Getting Rich'(1910)).

In addition to giving you practical tools and techniques, VISION will also help you to develop the mindset that enables you to achieve your goals.

Unless you are a hermit living in an isolated place miles from anywhere with no human contact, it is pretty certain that there are people in your life that it would be useful to have supporting you. As you move towards achieving your dreams and ambitions, here are some ways in which other people can help and guide you:

- You can ask them great questions to develop your thinking and refine your plan.

- They can ask you thought provoking questions.

- They can give you advice and practical support or pass on their expertise.

- They will encourage and motivate you when your energy is low.

- They will share your excitement and determination when your energy is high.

This demands their time and energy. No matter how willing they are to be involved, you will get the best from them if they:

- Understand your vision (they don't necessarily have to buy into it wholeheartedly).

- Can see and understand your reasoning.

- Are able to grasp the benefits.

If you don't truly understand your vision yourself (because you've not taken time give it sharpness and focus), you will communicate it less effectively. It will have less power for those around you.

'Imagining what you want as if it already exists opens the door to letting it happen.'

Shakti Gawain

Chapter TWO

VISION
Getting started with goals

'A goal is a dream with a deadline.'

Napoleon Hill

Getting Started with Goals

Why are some people really good at having a grasp of the big picture or a clear sense of direction?

Why do some people make their vision a reality and others don't?

What comes to mind?

In Stephen Covey's highly regarded book, 'The 7 Habits of Highly Effective People' (1989), habit 2 is to 'begin with the end in mind'. Developing your goals will be the preparation for you now, before you embark on the VISION system. What do you want and how are you going to get there?

In his book, Covey suggests the principle that all things are created twice:

Mental Creation - The vision (goal) of where you want to be and what you want to create. This is your imagination going to work.

Physical Creation - Make it happen – do something!

This chapter will help you to capture (or create) your goal. This works best if you take just one goal at this stage. This might be the most important goal for you right now. The size of that goal doesn't matter and can be from any area of your life. Where are you heading? Where do you want to be? What you want to be doing? What do you want to achieve?

Maybe you already have thoughts and ideas. If this is the case, the activities in this chapter will shape them for you and capture the detail. You might romp through these initial activities quickly. Alternatively, you might want to give more substantial thought to the future that you want to create. If so, set aside plenty of time for this chapter before you move on to the VISION system in chapter three.

Working with a partner or coach will tease out a depth of detail that you might not achieve on your own. Ask a partner to read the questions that follow and write down your answers for you. This will leave you free to do the thinking and imagining. Sit back and think about possibilities. When you think you've finished each question, ask it once more before moving on. It's surprising what pops out just when you thought there were no ideas and thoughts left.

Before you begin – what do you want?

The first exercise in this chapter will help you write a clear statement about your goal, using the PURE model.

The second exercise in this chapter is to work with your goal in more depth by completing the well formed outcome pattern. This originates from the original work of Bandler & Grinder in the mid 1970s.

The third exercise takes you through a guided imagery process so that you can begin to visualise your goal. The Collins Dictionary (2013) partly defines vision as 'the ability to perceive something not actually visible, as through mental acuteness or keen foresight'. The third and final exercise in this chapter will take your goal and start to develop this for you.

'A goal properly set is halfway reached.' Zig Ziglar

Stating your Goal

There are lots of different goal setting acronyms to help you state your goal. Here is a favourite of mine adapted from John Whitmore's book 'Coaching for Performance' (2002).

PURE

P - Positively stated and with positive intent.

U - Under your control.

R - Realistic and the right size for you to make happen.

E - Ecological and ethical.

Ecology in this context is the study of consequences. What and who else will be affected? In science, ecology is the study of the relationship between living organisms and their environment. In terms of your goal, this also makes sense. As human beings we are part of a human system. What other people do has an impact on us and our own actions impact upon others. The way we speak, behave and interact with other others has consequences. These consequences might be intended or unintended, positive or negative.

When you set yourself a goal, there will be an impact on others around you and it is worth checking that you are happy with this. Recently a client set a goal that involved moving to a new part of the country and hadn't thought through how her husband and children would feel. Another client wanted a period away from home travelling and hadn't fully appreciated the detrimental effect on family finances. In both these situations they went back to adjust their PURE goal statement to make it more realistic and in tune with others. This may not have happened without time for the ecology check at the end.

The first activity in this book will take you through adjusting your goal until it meets the PURE requirements.

Figure 1: The creation of a PURE goal statement

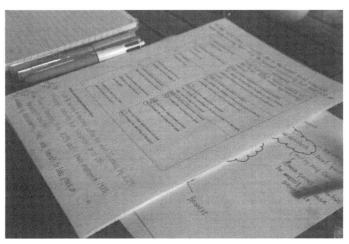

Activity 1 – State your Goal

Step 1 - Write your goal in the space below.

State your goal in terms of what you want and include your timescale or deadline for achieving it.

I want

_____

_____

_____

_____

Step 2 - Checking your goal with PURE

You will need some paper or a notebook for this step.

Use the template on the next page and adjust your goal using PURE criteria. Re-write your goal as many times as you like.

Write your final PURE goal statement here.

I want

_____

_____

_____

_____

Is your goal PURE?

	Instructions	Your responses
P	Write down your positive goal statement	I want…
U	Is achieving this goal under your control? Circle yes or no	No – Change the wording of the goal so that it reflects what you want in a way that is under your control. Yes – No further adjustment to the goal needed.
R	Is your goal realistic? Circle yes or no.	No – Change the wording of the goal so that it reflects what you want in a realistic way. Yes – No further adjustment needed.
	Is it the goal the right size for you to manage it and make it happen?	No – Change the wording of the goal so that it is the right size – not too big or too small. Yes – No further adjustment needed.
E	Could achieving this goal be harmful for yourself or others? Circle yes or no.	Yes – Change the wording of the goal. No – No further adjustment needed.
	Is anyone going to be adversely affected in a way that isn't acceptable?	Yes – Change the wording of the goal. No – No further adjustment needed.
	Is there any part of you that doesn't want to do this?	Yes – Change the wording of the goal. No – No further adjustment needed.

Creating a goal map

Now it's time to make a note of all the current thinking you have about your goal. What ideas have you thought about so far? What do you need? In the next activity you will develop in a visual pattern or Mind Map®. This is a divergent thinking tool that emerged from Tony Buzan's work on psychology and creative thinking. Visual maps are used for generating and recording ideas in a way that mirrors how the brain stores and retrieves information. Each line from the centre of the diagram represents a new idea and extra detail can branch off into sub sections.

A finished goal map might look something like the pictures and examples on the next few pages. Use them to guide you. Include as much colour as you like – your map can be simple or complex. The visual element is important because the mind works in images rather than words. The best maps will include pictures and doodles to illustrate the words and ideas being used. The key words in your goal map are used to trigger images in your neurology. The structure of your map shows the associations between words and pictures, mirroring the logic of your brain.

Activity 2 – Create a goal map

Step 1 - Take a plain piece of paper and write your goal in the middle.

Step 2 - Capture all your thoughts and ideas in a logical pattern. Each thought or idea will have a new branch.

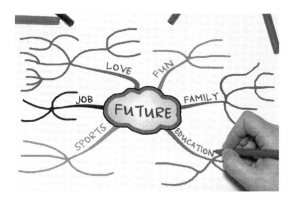

® *Mind Map is a trademark of the Buzan organisation*

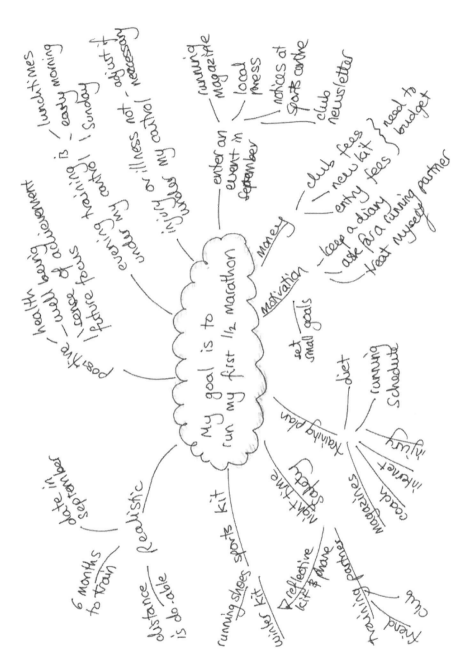

Figure 2: Helen's goal map

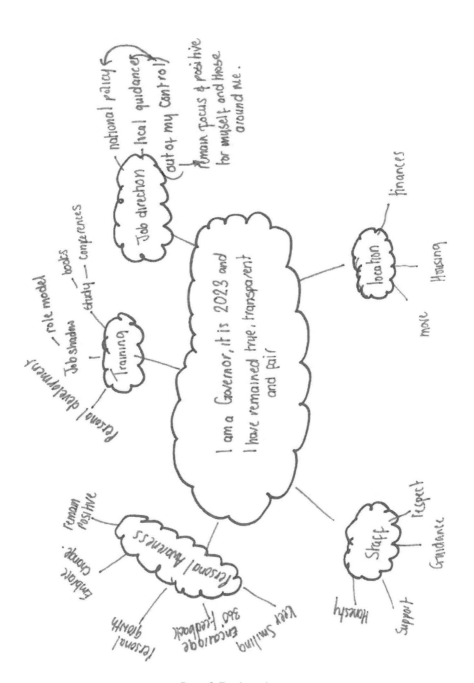

Figure 3: Terry's goal map

The Well Formed Outcome Pattern

Now you have prepared a goal statement and a goal map, it's time to add some more detail. The well formed outcome pattern (Bandler & Grinder 1981) will give your goal depth and make it robust. The basic questions in relation to your goal are:

- What do you want to see, hear and feel?

- Where do you want this?

- When do you want this?

- Who with?

- How will you know when you've got it?

- What will you see, hear and feel?

- What resources will you need?

You will be using these questions in activity 3 on page 43. You may repeat the questions as many times as you like in order to discover the widest range of possibilities. The best results come from using the questions without any adjustments, so resist the temptation to change them. The questions are designed to have linguistic patterns that firstly assist with the mental creation of your goal and secondly, presuppose success.

As with some of the other activities in this book, these questions will have the greatest impact if you work with a partner who can write down your answers for you. This gives you time and space to think and your partner will notice if you need to explore a question further or move on quickly. The beauty of this activity is that it can take just 10 minutes or over an hour, depending on how much time you have available. How long you spend developing your thoughts and responses to each question is up to you.

The six questions above create an overall representation of your goal that will have increased detail, substance and motivation. It will be well-formed.

What do you want to see, hear and feel?

Your internal representation of your goal (synaesthesia) will be structured using your three main senses of pictures (visual), sounds (auditory) and feelings (kinaesthetic), commonly known as VAK. You may even have a clear sense of taste (gustatory) or smells (olfactory) associated with your goal (VAK becomes VAKOG). These senses are important to you because through these, you take in and make sense of the world around you. You can also use these five senses to create a compelling representation of the future that you want.

You will probably have a clear preference for one or two of the senses. Discovering your VAKOG preferences can be very useful in constructing the goal in your mind. For example, if you have a strong kinaesthetic preference (feeling and doing), spend time writing down how achieving your goal will make you (and others) feel. If your least preferred sense is auditory, deliberately add in some extra sounds to your goal and notice if that brings your goal alive in a new and better way. If the sounds don't help or make the goal worse, take them out again. If you're not sure about your preference, include all the three elements of VAK to bring it alive.

The Cartesian Coordinate questions (figure 4) are the final four questions in the well formed outcome activity and they have an important part in the process.

1) Theorem: What will happen if I do (fully achieve my goal)? This creates visualisation of your goal.

2) Converse: What won't happen if I do (achieve my outcome)? Take time to answer this question as it helps you to think about what you might lose (for better or worse) by achieving your goal. Is there anything which will be lost that is important to you?

3) Inverse: What will happen if I don't (achieve my outcome)? This question is likely to bring about some discomfort in considering not achieving what you want and therefore increase the motivation for making it happen.

4) Non Mirror Image Reverse: What won't happen if I don't (achieve my outcome)? This question confuses and can make you aware of something that was previously hidden. You might gain a fresh perspective.

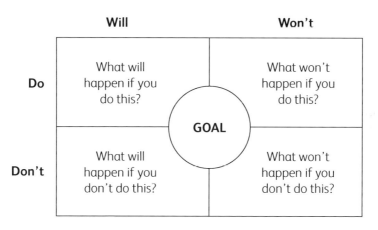

Figure 4: Cartesian Coordinate Questions

These four questions will check the ecology of your goal and stretch your thinking. Maybe you won't be able to give answers that make any logical sense at this stage and that doesn't matter right now. You can write down your responses, think about the answer in your head or, if there is no obvious answer to grab hold of, just consider the question and then move on. Any of these reactions will be fine. When you have finished considering your goal from all four angles, either the motivation to achieve it (and the VAK synaesthesia) will have strengthened or you will have discovered something that needs checking out before you continue (in which case go back to the first activity in this chapter and reconsider your goal against the PURE structure).

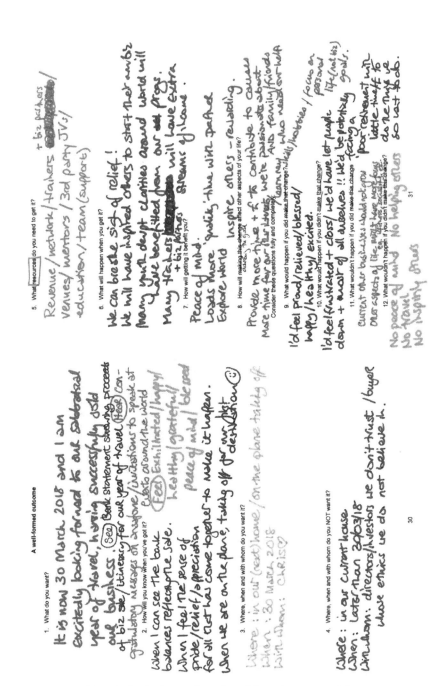

Figure 5: Caroline's notes from the well formed outcome activity

Activity 3 – The Well Formed Outcome Questions

1. **What do you want?**

I want…

What do you want to see?

What do you want to hear?

What do you want to feel?

Is there anything else about that?

2. **Where** do you want this?

3. **When** do you want this?

4. **Who** with?

5. **How will you know** when you've got it?
   What will you see, hear and feel?

6. **What resources** do you need?

What will happen if you do this?

What won't happen if you do this?

What will happen if you don't do this?

What won't happen if you don't do this?

Visualisation

In their book 'The Structure of Magic', Bandler and Grinder talk about the power of 'guided fantasy' as a way of creating a new experience and a new reference structure that takes you beyond past or current experiences. This means that by visualising having achieved your goal, you have a guide for the future you want and how you might get there.

Visualisation is widely used by actors, professional sports people and top business people. Visualisation will plant the seeds of the future in your mind and it is a rehearsal for achieving your goal. Sometimes called guided imagery, visualisation is safe and relaxing and it can help you to gain a clearer sense of what you want and you will become more motivated to make it happen. At this point you don't need to know how you will achieve your goal, but simply know what you want. This activity will strengthen the connection with the goal you developed in the well formed outcome (Activity 2) and allow you to imagine the experience of achieving it and the benefits it will bring you. Some people think that visualisation is supported by the law of attraction. Whatever you are thinking about you will notice more of, meaning that new opportunities and options will present themselves to you.

Maybe you have had the experience of buying a new car. As soon as you start to think about new cars, you suddenly notice adverts in the press, car sales forecourts or TV adverts that you've paid little attention to before. You might also start to notice more occurrences of the type of car you want as you are travelling on the roads. If you are looking for a five door family car, all of a sudden the roads seem to be full of them, in a wider range of styles and colours than you ever imagined. Holding a thought in your mind presents new opportunities.

Interestingly, as you start to think about the type of car you'd like to be driving right now, what comes to mind? It is unlikely to be words that you notice (do you see the letters r-e-d-c-o-n-v-e-r-t-a-b-l-e-s-p-o-r-t-s-c-a-r in your imagination or pictures?).

This is another reason why you will be working with pictures and images in this book – our neurology naturally prefers them

Using visualisation

In order to visualise, it is best to remove distractions and close your eyes. Unless you have superpowers and can read with your eyes shut, you will need to ask someone to read a visualisation script to you. Pauses are important as they allow you to develop the pictures in your mind. You could also record yourself reading the script out loud and then listen to an audio file on your MP3 player, phone or computer.

Here are some tips to make visualisation work really well:

- Find a quiet and private space.

- Get into a comfortable position where you can be still and peaceful.

- Allow your mind to stop thinking logically and trust your senses to create something new.

- Let your mind wander during the activity.

- Whatever comes to mind will be fine, even if it's not precise or exact.

Instructions for the person reading the script:

- Read the script word for word.

- '… ' indicates when it would be a good time to pause and let the other person just be still or think – more dots mean a longer pause.

- Read out loud in a calm, gentle and peaceful tone of voice – unhurried but not too slow as you still want to sound natural and yourself.

Activity 4 – Make your goal compelling with visualisation

> **Step 1** - How positive and motivated are you feeling about your goal at this moment? If you were to give that feeling a score out of 10, what would it be?
>
> **Step 2** - Listen to the guided visualisation below – ask someone to read it to you or pre-record it into an audio device.

Guided visualisation

"Close your eyes and relax .... Let's begin with a few slow deep breaths .... As you let go of each breath, release any tension or stress that you may be holding on to .... that's great .... As you feel yourself relaxing right now, notice a picture in your head of you having achieved the goal that you want .... Allow your imagination to create pictures of you being in this place .... Absorb yourself in the experience .... as if you are really there.

See achieving the goal as if you are in it .... Watching it through your own eyes. Notice everything around you as you know you've achieved your goal .... What can you see? .... What are you doing? .... Where are you? .... Who else is there? .... What else is going on? .... What are you feeling ....?

Make the pictures bigger and closer to you .... Imagine you have a remote control and turn up the intensity .... Change the colour and the contrast so that it is just right for you now .... the brightness .... the sounds .... Anything else that makes it more alive and a more powerful experience…

Maybe there are some smells that are important here .... or something you can taste…

Notice the increased intensity of all the different feelings you have now your goal has been achieved .... Turn it up some more to create the very best experience of what it will be like when you achieve this.

What are you thinking now that you have achieved that goal .... What are you saying to yourself ?

What are you saying to other people?

Take a little while longer to enjoy your sense of happiness, fulfilment or something else that you notice is powerful for you.

Now that you are thinking, hearing, seeing, and touching everything as you would if you were actually there, it's time to come back to now, knowing it can be as you want it to be.

When you are ready, open your eyes and come back into the present moment. Stretch and smile."

Step 2 - Reflection

Give your feelings of positivity and motivation towards your goal a new score out of 10. Refer to your score in step 1 – what has changed?

_____

_____

What is different about your goal in your mind now you have completed the visualisation exercise? What has changed when you think about your goal now?

_____

_____

This third activity (guided visualisation) is designed to take you to your goal as if you are actually in the moment of achieving it and seeing it through your own eyes. This is described as being associated with your goal. By stating the goal as if you are in it, and having achieved it, you can briefly imagine experiencing all the benefits.

Here is another way of looking at this principle:

"Imagine floating out of your body now and upwards, so that you are looking down on yourself reading this book. Float up higher still, so that you can see yourself sat there with this book below, smaller than before. Turn round and look into your future. From where you are, floating up high, look out into your future so that you can see it before you. As fast as you want to, float forwards into your future and notice as you look down below you, where the moment is that you are achieving your goal. When you are ready, drop down into that moment in time – you are there, achieving your goal. How do you know you have achieved it? What is happening? What can you see, hear, feel, smell or taste (VAKOG)? You are now associated with your goal.

When you are ready, you can leave that moment behind, knowing that it is there waiting for you. Take one last look around you and float up above your goal. You are now dissociating yourself. Turn back towards the present moment and notice all the steps you have taken to be here now, achieving what you want. When you are ready, float back towards now at the speed that allows you to preserve the learnings from this experience. When you are back, you will see yourself below sat reading this book. Drop down and come back into the present. Relax and smile."

By learning about your goal as if you are over there in the future and then coming back to the present day, it firstly enables you to check it out (make sure it's what you really want). Secondly, it leaves the goal 'out there' ready for you to make it happen in real life.

Activities 1 and 2 were firmly placed in the current state, in other words as you are in the here and now, thinking about the future in front of you some time ahead. Activity 3 took you briefly into the desired state.

The language of your goal statement can reflect this and you might have a preference for what sounds or feels better for you or looks good written down.

Present state - State your goal in terms of what you want in the future. This is being dissociated from your goal – imagine it is over there waiting for you.

Desired state - State your goal as if you have already achieved it. You are associated with your goal, meaning that you are in the moment experiencing it as if it was real. You have stepped into your future and you might be using a visualisation technique to imagine being there.

Here is a brief example:

Present State (dissociated) - 'I want to travel to Australia in January next year. I want to see the Great Barrier Reef and travel to a sheep station in the outback.'

Desired State (associated) - 'It is January next year. I am in Australia. I have just spent a few days at the Great Barrier Reef and I am about to start my journey to a sheep station.'

It is important to understand the difference between associated and dissociated in goal setting. If you can see, hear and feel the goal you are described as being associated with it. In your mind you are there experiencing your achievements as if they were real and the goal is giving you the feel good factor from being in that moment. However, your neurology thinks 'job done'. This can trick you into complacency about your goal, so beware! Why bother taking action if you can close your eyes, visualise and enjoy all the benefits in your mind without actually doing anything?

You need to be dissociated to be truly successful. This is possibly the greatest missing component where visualisation is used in goal setting. Visionary people get this bit right. If you dissociate yourself from the goal (stand back and see it over there in the future) you still have the power of seeing it and the steps that you need to take to get there, although the reward won't be yours until it is achieved. Therefore you are more compelled and motivated to take action.

Being associated with your goal in your mind probably won't stop you achieving it, although stepping away and becoming dissociated seems to be the difference that makes the difference.

You will definitely benefit from being associated with your goal at intervals. Put yourself back in the goal. Step into it as if you are there in real life having achieved what you want. See, hear and feel it fully (even smell it and taste it). Check it feels right. Then dissociate again and come back in the present time. See your goal ahead of you in the future and notice how it might seem a bit closer or more achievable now.

Summary

The three activities in this chapter have all worked to develop your goal and check that what you want is well formed and easily understood.

Vision is broader than merely wishing for something or having a goal. It is deeper than simply wanting more. It is the ability to see the future you want with amazing clarity. You can see plainly the steps you must take to get there.

"These activities were excellent for me. By breaking my goal down I feel more focussed and more empowered. I know that my goal is achievable and I will adapt my methods of approach and adopt new ones. I had never actually broken my goal down into bite size questions before which made me think about my direction and what would happen if I didn't achieve it – this isn't an option!"

– Terry

There is a difference between achieving goals or targets and creating an ambitious future by having a vision. You have now taken the first steps towards turning your goal into your vision. Vision provides a target for focus and a horizon for purpose.

"Would you tell me please which way I ought to go from here?"

"That depends a good deal on where you want to get to,"
said the Cat.

"I don't much care where," said Alice.

"Then it doesn't matter which way you go," said the Cat.

"So long as I get somewhere," Alice added as an explanation.

"Oh you're sure to do that," said the Cat,
"if only you walk long enough."

Alice in Wonderland

2 PART TWO

'Obstacles are those frightful things you see when you take your eyes off the goal.'

Henry Ford

Chapter THREE

VISION
An overview
of the system

'Dreams can become a reality when we possess a vision that is characterized by the willingness to work hard, a desire for excellence, and a belief in our right and our responsibility to be equal members of society.'

Janet Jackson

VISION – An overview of the system

This chapter gives you a quick reminder of the VISION system followed by a self assessment activity.

Step 1 - Values - In this first step you will uncover the important thing (s) about your vision for the future. It's about 'first things first'. Knowing this will help you to prioritise your efforts. There are several exercises to help you uncover and work with your values.

Step 2 - Identity - Knowing who you are in relation to your vision will be very powerful for you. This may be as simple as throwing out 'I'm not quite confident' and bringing in 'I can make it happen'. Some people see identity as the hats they are wearing in different areas of their life and others as their roles or jobs. Our identity is made up of 'I am ....' statements underpinned by beliefs about yourself. You will be thinking about which of these are going to be helpful and resourceful in achieving what you want.

Step 3 - Stories - You are going to need compelling evidence that your vision is the right thing to be working towards. You will need proof for yourself and proof that you can share with others. The stories that you tell can be very powerful in providing this proof and I will be giving you my DESERT and PEOPLE story-telling systems to help you achieve this.

Step 4 - Images - Visionary people have clear images in their mind of the future they want. These images have particular traits and qualities. This book will show you how to create the most useful images, both in your mind's eye for yourself and also in a way that you can describe or show to others.

Step 5 - Options - If you could do anything to make your vision happen what would it be? This step shares some great creativity techniques to increase the number of options available to you. The more options you have, the more flexibility you can exhibit when working with others and in overcoming challenges.

Step 6 - Next steps - Time for action planning. What specifically are you going to do next and what are the timescales for this?

Step 7 - Start and take steps - do something.

Before you begin with the first step, it is a good idea to pause and take stock.

At this stage, I would like you to take a 'snapshot' of where you think you are with the VISION system. When you bring your goal to mind and consider these seven steps, how would you rate your current level of understanding, skill and success? This is called a base line measure. You will begin with measuring where you are now and then compare your scores when you repeat this exercise at the end of the book. This will show you where the book has made the biggest difference and where to revisit activities to further develop your thinking.

A finished exercise might look something like Figure 6, with each part of the VISION system having been assigned a score.

Figure 6: VISION self assessment activity – an example

SCORE	Self assessment of the 7 VISION steps							SCORE
10 High								10 High
9								9
8				↑				8
7	↑				↑			7
6								6
5						↑	↑	5
4								4
3		↑						3
2								2
1								1
0 Low			↑					0 Low
	V	I	S	I	O	N	S	

Activity 1

Step 1 - Go back to the start of this chapter and read the descriptor for each step in VISION. Decide how well you are currently performing in each of the 7 steps and give yourself a mark out of 10 for each step. Make a note of your scores below.

	V	I	S	I	O	N	S
Score							

The highest scores would mean that on first impressions, you feel you are already extremely good at this aspect of the VISION system. A low score would mean that at the moment, you know very little or have few skills in this area. Don't worry if at this stage you are giving yourself a score based on limited understanding – just go with your instinct.

Step 2 - Use the template below to draw your scores with an arrow.

SCORE	Self assessment of the 7 VISION steps							SCORE
10 High								10 High
9								9
8								8
7								7
6								6
5								5
4								4
3								3
2								2
1								1
0 Low								0 Low
	V	I	S	I	O	N	S	

Below is a photograph of an alternative way of approaching the base-line scoring. The basic visual structure has been quickly drawn on a sheet of paper. Counters have been placed on the sliding scale from 0 -10 for each letter in the VISION system and the scores recorded. Paper, pens and counters are all you need for this activity.

Figure 7: Ashley's self assessment activity in action

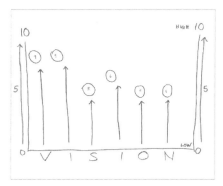

In the example above (Figure 7), stories, options and next steps appear to be the biggest area for development for this person as they work through the book. A strong sense of values and identity already coming through. I wonder what your initial assessment has shown?

Step 3 - Below there is some empty space for you to make notes. Record your thoughts in the way that suits you best. When you are ready, the next chapter will get you started with the detail of the VISION system.

Notes.

'Cherish your visions and your dreams as they are the children of your soul, the blueprints of your ultimate achievements.'

Napoleon Hill

Chapter FOUR

VISION
V is for Values

'What you drive isn't as important as what drives you.'

Source unknown

VISION – V is for Values

What is the most important thing for you?

If you could only achieve one thing in your vision for the future, what would it be? This is your core value. It is the reason you get up in the morning and work at achieving what you want. The reason you turn up for the day. It is the thing that motivates you to keep going, even when you are tired and facing difficulty or challenge.

What is the thing you are you putting first? Consider the first and most important reason for your motivation to work hard at this.

People with great vision have clear driving values and later in this chapter there is an exercise to help you to uncover yours. Your values guide your 'passion' or 'what matters'.

Wouldn't it be useful to know the core values that drive your vision so that you can communicate the message to others? If your core value is in the forefront of your mind, your passion and what matters will provide the motivation and energy for yourself and others around you. Awareness of your values will help you to set the rules for turning your vision into reality. Being clear about what is most important will give you the courage and strength to say 'no' to demands on your time and resources in less important areas.

Saying 'no' is one of the best time management tools available to us, although it's often one of the hardest things to do as we generally like to please others and do what we can to contribute and help. If you are clear about what is most important, you will achieve greater certainty about the best way to be spending your time and the reasons or justification for that. In turn, this will improve your delegation skills and time management skills. You will be better at deciding when to say 'yes', 'no' or 'maybe' to the demands of others around you.

When you value something, it is your energising and motivating force. Values give your goals deep-rooted meaning so you will be less likely to give up. You will be more likely to break through barriers, overcome obstacles and potential failures (R. L. Adams 2013). You will be more likely to create a reality from your vision and in a shorter period of time. For many people, values will surface as a gut instinct or your heart will tell you it's the right way to be going. Trust your instincts!

Values and Beliefs

Before moving on, it is worth distinguishing between values and beliefs. Often these two terms are used as meaning the same thing. Values are ideals that we hold to be important and they govern the way we behave, communicate and interact with others. Beliefs are concepts that we hold to be true and they are a bit like rules that we set for ourselves. For example, you might have a strong value around the importance of family in your life and then within this higher ideal or principle, you might have beliefs (rules) about what is important in achieving this, such as eating together at mealtimes, attending family celebrations whenever it's possible and having a holiday together every year. Values and beliefs determine our attitudes and opinions and they are the powerful motivating force for your vision. Values will inspire you.

The next activity will uncover the values that underpin your goal and begin the process of transforming your goal into a vision.

'Your vision will become clear only when you look into your own heart... Who looks outside, dreams; who looks inside awakes.' Carl Jung

Activity 1 – Uncovering your values

This activity works best if you have a partner who can take you through the questions and write down your answers for you. This will give you time, space and freedom from pen and paper to just think. If you are doing this activity alone, that will be fine too.

Step 1 - Re-state your goal from chapter two. Maybe you already have a clear vision for this goal and want to strengthen it; or perhaps you are starting from the beginnings of an idea that you wish to develop. Either is fine. Write your goal statement here:

Step 1 - **Goal statement** - I want…

_____

_____

_____

_____

Step 2 - Now create a short version of the goal statement in step 1 and write it in the gap below. This will turn it into a question.

What is important to me about…

_____

_____

_____

_____

_____

For example:

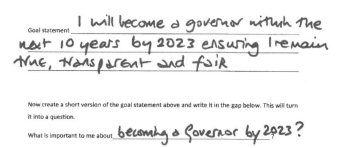

Goal statement: I will become a governor within the next 10 years by 2023 ensuring I remain true, transparent and fair

Now create a short version of the goal statement above and write it in the gap below. This will turn it into a question.

What is important to me about becoming a Governor by 2023?

If you are working with a partner, they will do all the writing and note taking. Your partner's job is to ask the questions and facilitate the exercise for you. The questions in this exercise are written as if you are working alone, so if you have a partner you will need to change the wording slightly for it to make sense when read aloud.

Step 3 - Ask the question you have completed for your goal (step 2) at least ten times. Record the words or phrases on cards. You will need about 15 slips of paper or card that are big enough to contain the phrase or sentence. All your ideas and responses to this question will be correct, as whatever you think or say instinctively will be the right answer. Write the answers down using the exact words and phrases that come to mind – they don't need to make sense to anyone else, only you.

As you do this activity, keep repeating the question in exactly the same way and exactly as you have written it in step 2. Resist the temptation to change or tweak the question. If you are working with another person, they should simply capture your exact words and phrases in quick succession.

I expect you will find the first five or six words or phrases came easily to mind. If you still have gaps, go back and ask yourself…

'What else is important to me about…?'

Keep going until no more answers are forthcoming and then ask the question a couple of times more – you'll be surprised what pops up! Aim for at least 10 completed cards and do a final check to eliminate any repetition.

Figure 8: Values hierarchy exercise

The cards you have created are your values for your goal.

Step 4 - Put your values in order of importance. If you could only have one thing on your list, what would it be? What would the next one be? What would the third on be? Lay out your cards on a flat surface in order of priority. Number one will be at the top. Keep going until all of them have been arranged in descending order.

I expect your new list is in a different order compared to the original order of your thoughts as they were written down. For some people that can be quite a dramatic change. Often, the last couple of ideas turn out to be the most important ones. This is why it can be helpful to work with a partner who keeps you thinking beyond the point at which you might have otherwise stopped.

If you have more than a ten cards at this stage, you'll find step 5 will take a long time and can get unwieldy. Remove the lower cards, leaving just the top 10.

Step 5 - The last part of this exercise is to check the rank order of your values. Look at the top card and the one beneath it (values 1 and 2). Maybe pull them slightly to one side as shown in the photo below and visually separate them from the rest of the list.

Ask yourself 'If I could only have one of these values, which one would it be?'

Remember you are being asked to make a choice as part of the exercise. In real life you can of course have both values. Just imagine here that you can only have one. Either the first one or the second one. Which would it be? Does number 1 need to swap places with number 2 on your list?

Now separate numbers 2 and 3 by moving them to one side. Ask yourself 'if I could only have one of these, which would I choose?'. Do numbers 2 and 3 need to swap rank order? If number 3 moves to number 2, then you will need to check your new number 1 against your new number 2 as there might need to be another change needed.

Continue checking in this way down your list. Number 3 against number 4 and so on. If any value moves up your list, you will need to go back to the one above and start double checking again. Sometimes a value lower down can jump up several places.

There may be a couple of values that are at the bottom of your top 10 which you begin to feel aren't really needed or relevant. If this happens, you can remove them.

Figure 9: Values hierarchy exercise – checking number 3 against number 4

Step 6 - When you are satisfied with the final number and order of your values, write them down or take a photograph. You could stick the cards in order on a sheet of paper and scan your work. If you are working with another person, take the pen from your partner and record the final list in your own handwriting and style. This gives ownership back to you and can be empowering. It also combines sensory input (your eyes) with motor input (your body), which is thought to accelerate learning.

Figure 10: Values hierarchy exercise – final rank order

It might help to read your list out loud or hear someone read it to you. Maybe display your list somewhere prominent at home or work, such as on a notice board or in the front cover of your diary or a notebook.

According to R. L Adams (1983), there are five key values which will act as motivators when attached to your goals:

- Family
- Freedom
- Faith
- Survival
- Love

Do you want to adjust your list of values to reflect anything on this list?

Now you know what is important to you about your vision. You also know what is most important and what is least important to you. This can be a huge help in prioritising your time and energy. Maybe you can do more tasks and activities to support what is higher up your list and less activity that supports what is lower down in your values?

Step 7 - Reflection

How are you thinking differently now you have completed this exercise?

_____

_____

What have you noticed about what is important to you?

_____

_____

Has anything changed?

_____

_____

Are there any values in your list that are holding you back from getting what you want? If so, remove them and see what happens.

_____

_____

'Try not to become a person of success, but rather to become a person of value.' Albert Einstein

Take a look at your finished hierarchy of values and notice if your values are 'towards' or 'away' values.

'Away from' values are expressed in terms of avoiding something and tend to be stated negatively (what you don't want). 'Towards' values will be goal focussed. If you notice any 'away from' values, re-word the statements – keep the meaning and adjust them to give them positive intent. For example, a project could be important because you will avoid disappointment – what is the positive opposite of this? Perhaps it is important that instead of avoiding disappointment, you will be fulfilled. Where you make changes, notice the impact this has on your motivation to succeed.

What is important to you – a mission statement

Now you have uncovered your values in relation to your goal, it would be useful to have a way of communicating these with people around you. A good format for doing this is a mission statement.

Your mission statement will be short enough to capture the essence of what is important to you and in a way that can be described to others with meaning and personal power.

Here are a couple of great examples of corporate mission statements:

Freecycle's mission is to build a worldwide gifting movement that reduces waste, saves precious resources & eases the burden on our landfills while enabling our members to benefit from the strength of a larger community.

Apple is committed to bringing the best personal computing experience to students, educators, creative professionals and consumers around the world through its innovative hardware, software and Internet offerings.

Activity 2 – Writing your mission statement

Step 1 - Put to one side your top 5 values from the previous exercise. These are the values that you are going to be working with to create your mission statement.

Step 2 - Use the instructions below to complete the sentences given to you. You should include some of the words and phrases in your top 5 values in these sentences. The examples in this section will also help you.

Firstly, think about the essential action and how you engage the world in relation to your goal. A useful way to start this is with 'I want to create......'. The grammar might not seem quite right straight away and you might end up with a slightly different sentence later in the process. Complete the sentence below to start you off in the right direction:

I want to create

_____

_____

Secondly, where is the focus of your attention (your central concern) and who will benefit (who is most directly affected)?

I want to create

_____

for _____

to affect _____

_____

Thirdly and finally, what is the intended impact or the immediate outcome?

I want to create

_____

for _____

to affect _____

_____

Now you have drafted your mission statement. Refine this statement until it encompasses your behaviour and experience. It is OK to change the wording of these templates slightly to fit your context. You may need to create several drafts and be patient in getting it just as you want it. You will know when it is right. The person working on the example in the photograph below knew when she had finished because she said 'I've gone all goose pimply with this experience!' The photo below shows a mission statement being created in this way, followed by the final result on the next page.

Figure 11: Writing a mission statement

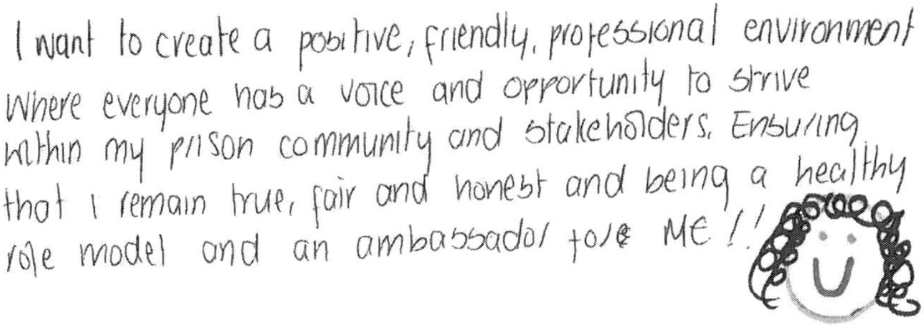

I want to create a positive, friendly, professional environment where everyone has a voice and opportunity to strive within my prison community and stakeholders. Ensuring that I remain true, fair and honest and being a healthy role model and an ambassador for ME !!

Figure 12: Terry's mission statement

Now, use this list from John Kotter's work on leading change (1996) to check that your written mission statement is as effective as it can be. Your mission statement should be:

- **Imaginable**

- **Desirable**

- **Feasible**

- **Focused**

- **Flexible**

- **Communicable**

How does your mission statement measure up against Kotter's checklist?

_____

_____

_____

_____

Write your final mission statement in the space below. Maybe you would like to use colour, symbols or other doodles and illustrations to bring it to life.

'Some of the world's greatest feats were accomplished by people not smart enough to know they were impossible.'

Doug Larson

Chapter FIVE

VISION
I is for Identity

'You attract what you are, not what you want.
So if you want it then reflect it!'

Tony Gaskins

VISION – I is for Identity

In the first few sections of this book you have gained a better understanding of your goal and why your goal is important. You are important too!

Ask yourself the question 'Who am I…? This question will give you labels for some of the identities by which you respond to the world. When you are connected with yourself and have clear sense of who you are (your identity), you are more likely to be authentic and true to yourself. By spending some time thinking about and developing who you are, you will become more focussed on achieving what you want and more resourceful in how you go about it. You will also communicate a clearer message to others that will originate from a deeper place within you and therefore have more meaning and power. This can also increase your charisma, which will be discussed later in this chapter.

In this chapter, the second step of the VISION system, there are six activities that will help you to connect with your inner self, especially those parts of you that will strengthen and support you in achieving your goal. Who are you and what do you stand for in relation to your goal? When you look in the mirror do you see someone who is the most effective person they can be in relation to their goals or somebody else?

Visionary people have a clear sense of who they are. This doesn't mean that they are perfect, arrogant, super confident or super human in any way. Quite the opposite in fact. Their strength is that they say to themselves 'This is who I am and these are the parts of me that will make happen what I want (or need) to make happen. I am a person **who can** do this. I am a person **that will** do this'.

Activity 1 Mirror, mirror...

When you look at yourself in the mirror in the morning, who is the person looking back at you? What are the 'I am........ 'statements that you say to yourself, or that you say to others. We have lots of different personas (the characters we play). Write these down in space provided below (I have given you a list of my own to give you some initial ideas).

Me	You
I am a mother	I am…
I am a daughter	
Friend	
Author	
Trainer	
Coach	
Sportswoman	
Administrator	
Plus lots more…	

The list you have given includes many of the different senses that you have of yourself. These are some of the identities (your roles in life) that define you. Which are the most important identities that will help you to get what you want?

Irene lives in my local area and she has recently set up a new business as an HR advisor. Here are some of the 'I am…' statements that she said to me within the first ten minutes of meeting her at a networking event recently:

- I am restricted by a disability…

- I am disorganised and in a mess…

- I am passionate about my new business…

- I am irritated by demanding customers…

- I am struggling to settle to work at my computer each day…

- I am someone who has been affected badly by recent redundancy…

Some of these statements support her in her new business and others have the potential to sabotage her achieving her best results. The 'I am…' statements were having an impact on her inner state and listening to them was draining and wearisome. Irene's social network postings also come across as negative and moaning. Maybe she has been having an unintended negative effect on her customers (or potential customers)?

'I am…' statements are like wearing hats – they can be taken off and put to one side if they are not fit for purpose. You can have them back whenever you want to wear them again.

- Firstly notice when you are using an 'I am…' statement.

- Secondly make a choice about whether to keep it as helpful or reject it as unhelpful.

- Thirdly, create some new 'I am…' statements to use in a specific situation to support your vision. The exercises in this chapter will help you to do this.

These are the new 'I am…' statements that Irene is now committed to using each day in order to project professionalism and passion in all her business dealings.

- I am supportive and professional.

- I am a business woman.

- I am passionate about my new business.

- I am organised and focussed at work.

- I am able to choose to rest and have time to myself when my disability is at its worst.

- I am a person who looks forward.

Irene has now changed the tone of her social networking posts, with a new focus on using professional language instead of personal comment. She now supports other businesses with ideas or advice via Facebook and Twitter and has stopped using her business profiles for off loading private frustrations with her disability and illness.

'I am…' is a statement of our identity and our self image. For example, if you want to achieve great things as a parent, will a strong identity of 'I am a manager at work' help you to achieve this? Possibly not, as you could be motivated to spend time working at home in the evenings or weekends which therefore takes energy, time and attention away from family. Apply this principle to achieving what you want. Develop a powerful vision and then communicate your vision with energised and enthused 'I am…' statements. Now consider having a mix of conflicting or un-resourceful identities and notice how it will dilute your drive and message.

Let me give you an example of confused identity and the impact this can have, from earlier in my career as a middle manager. My situation involved a new promotion from being in a team to leading the team. You may have experienced this yourself. In the early days of being a new middle manager I was still clinging on to my identity as a team member. In the past this had enabled me to pull together with other members of the team to achieve what we wanted. I socialised with the team, had the odd moan about senior leaders and a grumble about less welcome changes that were taking place. This didn't prove troublesome in my new role, until it became time to make a strategic decision that was unpopular. I didn't do a very good job of being clear and assertive with a couple of reluctant colleagues who were presenting me with performance management issues. This was a result of my identity being more in tune with team members rather than team leader.

This experience taught me an important lesson. In my new position there were new behaviours and responsibilities that I needed to embrace in order to be an effective manager. The first of these involved adopting a new identity. I started to spend more time with other middle and senior managers and I distanced myself from negative conversations over coffee in the staffroom. I began to dress slightly differently as this helped me to 'feel' the part and gave me a little more confidence when I was interacting with my new senior colleagues.

Visionary people are very clear about who they are within the context of their life circumstances. Their 'I am…' statements aren't just spoken. You can tell from their body language, how they speak, what they speak about and from their demeanour and presence. They frequently talk about their vision and achieving their dream. They say 'yes' or 'no' to requests from others based upon who they are in a given situation and how this is to be played out. Their strong sense of identity come across and gives instils total confidence in others. They know who they are and what their role is in making something amazing happen.

The next few activities will support you to develop your identity further, so that you are thinking and feeling in the way that supports your vision in the best way possible. The words that you say will affect your thoughts, feelings, emotions and body language. Most importantly they will affect your focus and resourcefulness In achieving what you want.

> *"Working through the activities in this chapter reaffirmed who I am and my positive outlook. Negative thoughts are a drain on my energy and interrupt my work flow. Remembering who I am will help me to know where I am going."*
>
> – Mike

Activity 2

Re-state what you want (your goal). I want…

_____

_____

_____

_____

Go back to activity 1 and look at your list of 'I am…' statements. Take the best version(s) of 'you' from the list. These are the 'I am…' statements that are resourceful or will support you in pursuit of your goal. Write them again here. I am…

_____

_____

_____

_____

Now complete this sentence:

To get what I want, the best version(s) of me is…

_____

_____

_____

_____

Now consider how much time (up until this moment) that you have spent thinking in that identity and being that person. Are you being the person you need to be, enough of the time, to get what you want?

Now take a look back through activities 1 and 2. Did you write down your name on any of the lists? Did you write the word 'me'? Maybe I tricked you slightly as I didn't write my name on the list either. However, 'you' are the most important identity you have and the label for 'you' is your name. Behind that name (internally within you) are all of your inner strengths and abilities. All the other identities or personas on your list are probably the things other people judge you by. Other people have an opinion about your effectiveness in those roles. These are the things against which you are judged that can affect your confidence and self belief. The labels have standards and desired behaviours that are imposed on you.

However, it's OK to be 'you'. It is OK to be who you are, to be what you want to be and to set out to achieve that in a way that benefits yourself and others around you (within ethical, moral and legal boundaries).

What is the very best version of you?

How can you be that person more often in the pursuit of your dreams and goals?

It is important to be authentic and true to who you really are. Within that authenticity, it is possible to change your behaviours and reactions and wear a different 'hat' according to the demands of different areas in your life. Adopting different and appropriate identities can increase your personal effectiveness in different situations.

Congruence is extremely important. Being congruent means all the parts of you fit together, so that you are consistent with what is happening within yourself and with your interactions with the rest of the world. Identity isn't about putting on an 'act' or creating something that isn't true to who you are. If you do put on an act, it is likely that you will be found out and this will reduce the level of trust that others have in you.

There are several versions of you and they are all you, yet with subtle differences. Whilst I was as teacher for example, I can remember my husband saying to me, 'will you stop talking to me as if I am one of your pupils'. In this instance I had brought the 'teacher' version of me home and forgotten to put it away! It would also be inappropriate for you to take the 'relaxed at home' version of you into an important work presentation or the 'I am out at the pub for the evening' version of you into a meeting!

I am aware that there are subtle differences in my identity between delivering a training day to teachers and delivering almost exactly the same day to a group of executives from a high end car manufacturer. My language is slightly different, what I wear is slightly different and even how I stand and move around is slightly different, and maybe more importantly, my focus on who I am is slightly different. Identity is important and identities are fit for purpose in different situations.

Case study - Alison's garden

Four years ago the builders had finished renovating Alison's house and the garden was a sea of mud. She had a picture in mind (and sketched on a piece of paper) for what she wanted to achieve. Alison knew she could afford to buy the basic resources, but couldn't afford to engage a specialist landscape gardener. She definitely was not an expert in plants, horticulture or landscaping, yet she still made something wonderful happen on a small scale. How did Alison do it? Well, the lists opposite show the identities Alison used and the identities that she pushed to one side for a short period of time to stop them getting in the way.

Alison's gardening project	
Helpful identities	**Unhelpful identities**
I am...	**I am not...**
Alison, me, sure of myself	Mother and wife
Certain this is going to work (I know)	Cook and cleaner
Hardworking and organised	Dog walker
Determined and intrepid	Company director
Flexible	Relaxed, caring & nurturing

Alison was congruent with all the helpful identities above as she had experienced them all before in genuine situations. None of them were an 'act' or going against what she valued as important. All of the helpful identities in the left hand column were brought in from other areas of her life and applied to her gardening project. For example, she could remember a work project in the past where she had a very tight deadline, which she only achieved because of hard work, longer hours than normal and a narrow, sharp focus.

Alison chose to push some of the other identities to one side because they were in conflict with what she wanted at that time. They are still hugely important identities for her and she only removed them temporarily. Alison sought agreement from the people who would be affected. She said to her family something along the lines of 'I am going to spend the next couple of days in the garden and leave you all to fend for yourselves at meal times. Is that OK?'

Once she had explained her goal for the weekend with passion and enthusiasm, stating that she needed help and support and promised (to herself and others) that after a few days things would be back to normal, it was surprisingly easy. Nobody thought less of her.

Sometimes we hold back from doing what we really want because of a misplaced sense of loyalty. How we might be judged (going back to the labels that others give us) and the 'I am indispensable' mentality can get in the way. This is where the ecology check from chapter one is useful. Not only can it prevent unintended negative consequences from embarking on something new, it can also keep us firmly in our place and prevent us generating an inflated sense of importance in everyone else's lives. When Alison stopped and examined the impact of pursuing her gardening goal for a weekend, there wasn't really much negative impact at all.

Activity 3

Begin to sort out the identities that support you or hinder you.

Step 1 - State your goal (what you want) in the first box.

Step 2 - Complete the list of helpful identities that you are going to engage with more often when you are working on your goal.

Step 3 - Complete the list of unhelpful identities that you could choose to put to one side. Maybe they could get in the way or reduce your effectiveness.

I want...	
Helpful identities	**Unhelpful identities**
I am...	**I am not...**
I am the kind of person who…	I am not…
At my best in this situation I am…	At my worst I am…

Activity 4

What are you going to stop saying to yourself about who you are?

Stop saying I am…

_____

_____

_____

_____

Sometimes it is helpful to learn from the experts. There may be new identities that you would like to adopt that you've never experienced before. Perhaps you have no prior understanding of what an identity sounds, looks or feels like. For example, sometimes people say 'I've never been a confident person'. In this instance, think about another person who is confident and effective – maybe they are from history, family, literature, business, sport or the world of celebrity. In relation to your goal, maybe you have somebody in mind who is technically an expert or they have other qualities and attributes that have enabled them to achieve something similar (or the same as) your goal.

Who can you think of right now that has achieved something fantastic by using personal qualities that you would like to have more of (such as determination, confidence, assertiveness, common sense etc). Maybe they achieved exactly the same thing as you have stated in your goal, or maybe something completely different and you admire them as an 'achiever'. What do you think their identities were in their situation? What were the hats that they were wearing? When they looked in the mirror in the morning, who do you think they saw looking back that set them up to be effective each day?

This is a great modelling exercise for younger people who have less life experiences of their own to draw upon, or for someone who is seeking to operate completely out of their sphere of prior experience. Before you answer the questions below, have some thoughts in your mind about effective people. Remember they could be from sport, business or television - fictional or real. They are people who have 'I am…' statements that enable them to effective in their field.

Activity 5 – Stepping into the shoes of another person

Step 1 - Write your goal statement here. I want…

_____

_____

_____

Step 2 - Write down the name of a person (s) who you admire because they have qualities that you would like to have more of yourself.

_____

_____

_____

Step 3 - Imagine their 'I am…' statements and write them here:

_____

_____

_____

Step 4 - Choose one of the 'I am…' statements you have written down and say it to yourself (out loud or in your head) in the way that person would say it.

Notice what that sounds like and feels like for you.

What are you seeing through their eyes (with clarity and focus) as you say it?

Stand or sit as that person would stand or sit. In other words, try it on and adopt their physiology.

Make any other adjustments that you need to make to step into the shoes of that person and say the 'I am…' statement again (out loud or to yourself in your head).

Now you know how that sounds, feels and looks for you. Now carry out an ecology check. Ask yourself these questions:

- Could adopting this identity be harmful for me or others?

- Is anyone going to be adversely affected in a way that isn't acceptable?

- Is there any part of me that doesn't want to be this person?

Now test your new identity statement(s) one final time – say 'I am…' to yourself and notice what happens.

This technique is a stimulus response, often called an anchor. In step 4 of this exercise you have given yourself a picture (V), sound (A) and feeling (K) for the identity of a person who has qualities that would be useful to you. This is training your mind and emotions to take on that identity. It is possible to improve the strength of its impact for you, just through practice. Consciously you know that it's not real experience. The great thing is that neurologically and sub-consciously your body can't tell that it's only imagined, so you really are practising and getting 'in the zone' in a way that is useful.

You can take charge of the imagery and statements that happen in your mind. Just like seeds in a garden, these will germinate and grow.

Step 5 - Setting up your simple anchor.

In step 4 you created a VAK (visual, auditory and kinaesthetic) representation for the successful mindset of an achiever and you adopted their mindset (their body language, their words and their pictures). Now you can have that back whenever you want by creating a trigger. These are used widely in sport and business as a focus for peak performance. The Maori Haka at the start of an All Blacks (New Zealand) international rugby match is a trigger for powerful team spirit and aggression and Jonny Wilkinson (England International 1998-2011) has a famous stance that he adopts before kicking a penalty or conversion which triggers in his mind the sounds and images of a successful kick between the posts before it has even happened. Many major speakers and presenters have stage anchors so they can create confidence and overcome natural nerves and apprehension.

You have already established a simple auditory anchor in step 4 by practising saying 'I am…' to yourself. You have noticed how that brings back the feeling and pictures of being an achiever. You can strengthen this simply by repetition. You can also use a physical stimulus, such as touching your thumb and finger together or clenching your fist when you state 'I am…'. With repetition of this exercise, you will quickly reach the point where just touching your finger and thumb together will quickly access the pictures, words and feelings of the identity you want.

Setting an anchor in this way can help you to access your desired identity or any other positive emotional state that will support you. Anchors can be also be visual, olfactory or gustatory.

> *"When I go to work I wear Avon's Pure Gold perfume. For day-to-day activity I wear Tommy Hilfiger and when I go out in the evening I wear Black Moon. My different perfumes help to trigger my different identities in these areas of my life."*
>
> – Emma

Charisma

Charisma is an interesting concept to introduce here, as by strengthening your useful identities you may also develop increased charisma. Dictionary definitions mention charm and appeal as being qualities of charismatic people. They tend to influence and inspire others in a way that is powerful. Charismatic people that I have met over the years, in all walks of life, have a high level of self confidence and assurance that is never arrogant and is always warm and gracious. I believe that spending time on developing your identity can also contribute to creating personal charisma. Your personal presence in relation to your goal will grow as your identity strengthens. Belief in who you are (a strong identity) will create a special aura. This makes your choice of identities important if you want to inspire and motivate others.

If your personal presence becomes over confident, arrogant or conceited, you are likely to alienate or intimidate people, which isn't great if you want their support and encouragement in helping you to achieve your goals.

This was brought home to me recently when I was sat in the waiting room at an out patients' clinic at a local hospital. Two consultant surgeons were coming and going from reception. Neither of them wore name badges, however it was obvious to me they were consultants because of their presence – a combination of how they dressed, walked and spoke.

Both had presence, but only one had charisma. The first of these consultants came across as arrogant and his identity as a surgeon from where I was sat was a bit like 'I am a consultant and I am superior'. He didn't make eye contact with anyone, didn't smile and wore his stethoscope round his neck like a status symbol. He also had metal segs on the heels of his shoes which clicked and clacked on the floor as he walked, announcing his arrival and departure. The reception staff were very frosty with him and they didn't go an inch out of their way to help him when he came and asked to borrow some sticky tape in rather a gruff manner.

The second consultant surgeon also had great presence, even though he was smaller in stature. As he walked confidently past reception a few minutes later (quietly and with his stethoscope in his pocket) he paused, smiled, asked for a pen and thanked the staff for bringing him a cup of tea earlier in the afternoon. His identity came across as 'I am a consultant and I am also a human being just like you.' The receptionist stopped what she was doing to engage with him and another looked out from the back office just to say hello. He elicited a much more positive reaction.

The swan is a great metaphor for charisma. The second consultant in my anecdote above had something of the swan about him, whilst the first was maybe more like a peacock in the way he strutted around and flaunted his presence.

The impressive stature, charm and elegance of this swan reminds us why the bird became a status symbol and was given royal status in the 12th century. Beneath the surface the feet of a swan are working hard as they paddle and steer to get to where they want to be, whilst on the surface their progress seems to happen with ease and grace. The most visionary and inspiring people are just like the swan. However, the moral of the Arrogant Swans story below adds a note of caution.

The Arrogant Swans

In a far away kingdom, there was a river. This river was home to many golden swans. The swans spent most of their time on the banks of the river. Every six months, the swans would leave a golden feather as a fee for using the lake. The soldiers of the kingdom would collect the feathers and deposit them in the royal treasury.

One day, a homeless bird saw the river. "The water in this river seems so cool and soothing. I will make my home here," thought the bird.

As soon as the bird settled down near the river, the golden swans noticed her. They came shouting. "This river belongs to us. We pay a golden feather to the King to use this river. You cannot live here."

"I am homeless, brothers. I too will pay the rent. Please give me shelter," the bird pleaded. "How will you pay the rent? You do not have golden feathers," said the swans laughing. They further added, "Stop dreaming and leave at once." The humble bird pleaded many times. But the arrogant swans drove the bird away.

"I will teach them a lesson!" decided the humiliated bird.

She went to the King and said, "Oh King! The swans in your river are impolite and unkind. I begged for shelter but they said that they had purchased the river with golden feathers."

The King was angry with the arrogant swans for having insulted the homeless bird. He ordered his soldiers to bring the arrogant swans to his court. In no time, all the golden swans were brought to the King's court.

"Do you think the royal treasury depends upon your golden feathers? You cannot decide who lives by the river. Leave the river at once or you all will be beheaded!" shouted the King.

The swans shivered with fear on hearing the King. They flew away never to return. The bird built her home near the river and lived there happily forever. The bird gave shelter to all other birds in the river. (Valeti 2011).

Take a few moments to reflect on the story of the arrogant swans.

Take the best attributes of the swan (grace, elegance, working hard whilst making it look effortless) and apply them to your own behaviours in relation to your goal.

In developing your personal charisma, what would it be useful to...

Start doing

_____

_____

_____

_____

_____

_____

Stop doing

_____

_____

_____

_____

_____

_____

Below is a charisma development model (Wikihow):

- Relax.

- Look confident through body language and behaving as an equal to others.

- Develop a warm personality.

- Get in touch with your emotions and with other people's.

- Match your body language to your speech – be genuine.

- Think before you speak – less is more – silence is fine.

- Speak with conviction.

- Treat people as you want to be treated – listen actively and make other people feel special.

Plus:

- Charisma must come from within you as an individual – individuality is vital.

- Everyone can be charismatic.

- Have a message, which can be controversial.

- Be honest and bold, but don't offend people.

What combination of 'I am…' statements might you create so that you strengthen your identity and presence in a way that gives others confidence and belief in your goal and your ability to achieve it? Get this right and you will have magic at your fingertips.

Using perceptual positions to strengthen your identity

Perceptual positions (see figure 12 below) is a technique that involves the skill of adopting more points of view than your own. In its simplest form, it works like this:

First Position - You, fully involved in achieving your vision; a position of personal strength. The downside is that you might lack understanding of others and push to achieve what you want without considering the consequences.

Second Position - Walking, seeing, hearing, feeling and thinking in another person's shoes. You will be aware of the emotions and thinking of others. You can consider different perspectives and reactions or seek opinion.

Third Position - You are an observer of the other two. Sometimes this is called the 'friendly visitor from outer space who has just arrived' position! This is the place where you notice more complex patterns and interactions. Here you can take a detached perspective and check the wider ecology of your outcomes, remove personal emotions (yours and others) and find solutions to problems.

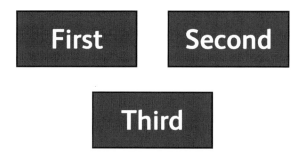

Figure 13: The Perceptual Positions model

This model was developed by John Grinder and Judith de Lozier (1987) who discovered that successful negotiators were able to find a win-win situation through adopting the perspectives of others.

This chapter has shown you how a strong sense of identity is important in achieving your vision – this can be likened to being in first position in the model. In the first position you will be very aware of yourself (and your values). It is still important to enter the second position and check out the perspectives and opinions of others as this will help you to fine tune your vision and check out its wider impact. It will also give you the opportunity to consider how best to appeal to other people by finding out what might motivate them to support you.

In order to share your vision, lead change and create the future you want, you will need to return to first position. This is because you will have personal strength here. You will be in touch (associated) with your motivations, skills, abilities, values and purpose - your sense of identity will be clear. Weaker people, those whose vision gets watered down or it never quite happens, remain in second position for longer. In second position you might compromise your own dreams and desires in order to fit in more with the views and goals of others. You might even lose respect. Visionary people are very clear about their great ability to return to first position to take action. Whilst utilising and recognising the value of second and third positions, you will consciously return to first position and spent most time here.

Being in first position isn't selfish unless that is your only view of the world. I am pretty sure you will want to take others on the journey with you and not ride roughshod over all the people in your life. You will seek their views, consider their needs, imagine how your plans will affect them (for better or worse) and adapt your own thoughts accordingly. You will need to enter second position to do this effectively. Stay there briefly or you will get waylaid by other people's agendas to the detriment of your own vision. Go into third position and take a pragmatic and impartial view – briefly step back (dissociate) and consider the whole system and everything going on around you. Check out the wider consequences, benefits and results. Stay detached for just a short time or you could lose the personal passion and determination to do what you know is right. The downside of third position can be 'sitting on the fence', which is a place where not a lot happens and that's not what you want, is it?

Activity 6 below is an exercise to explore and develop your VISION by taking you through the principles of perceptual positions. You will begin and end with first position, whilst gathering useful information from other people and the wider system. This activity was developed by Robert Dilts (1992) and is commonly referred to as the Meta Mirror. The activity works best with floor cards, giving you a physical space to stand (on the floor) for each position and where each position is separated from the others. When you move between each place on the floor it will help you to change state and enter a new perspective with new thinking. As with many of the activities in this book, having a partner to take you through the questions will leave you free to think and process what comes to mind, which can sometimes create better results than doing it on your own. Reading the activity alone and noting down your thoughts is another approach you could take.

Activity 6 – The Meta Mirror

Firstly, create three floor cards and lay them out like this:

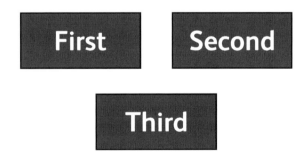

State your goal out loud or write it down here:

> I want…
>
> _____
>
> _____

Step 1 - Stand in first position. Look at the other people involved in achieving your vision in second position.

- What are you seeing when you look at these people?

- What sounds and words do you hear?

- What do you sense or feel about these people?

Step 2 - Move and stand in second position and look back at yourself in first position. If it helps, imagine stepping into the shoes of other people one at a time (or as a group). Pretend you have left yourself behind in first position over there.

Now that you are stood in the shoes of others – what are you thinking and feeling as you look back at you?

Step 3 - Complete this written activity:

> Now that I am…
> *(write the name of the person or group in the gap above)*
>
> what am I thinking about… *(write your name here)*?
>
> _____
>
> _____
>
> _____

Now that I am…
(write the name of the person or group in the gap above)

what do I want to ask   *(write your name here)?*

_____

_____

_____

Now that I am…
(write the name of the person or group in the gap above)

what is my/our positive intention?

_____

_____

_____

Now that I am…
(write the name of the person or group in the gap above)

is there anything else about that?

_____

_____

_____

It is important that the language you are using in the gaps above reflects the fact that you are stood 'over there' as if in the shoes of others. You are looking back at yourself and writing thoughts and feelings as if you are the other people.

Step 4 - Move and stand in third position. You can see both yourself and the other people over there. Feel free to analyse the situation from here.

- As an independent observer, how are you responding to you, over there in first position?

- Is there anything you want to tell that person or ask them?

- What advice would you offer 'you' over there?

Step 5 - Go back to second position and ask 'what has changed?'

Step 6 - Go back to first position and ask 'what has changed?'

Step 7 - Now consider the following:

- Stay in first position and notice all your strengths.

- Stay in first position and notice the values for achieving what you want.

- Who are you stood here right now?

- What is your purpose?

- What is important to you and what do you believe in?

- Gather up your skills and abilities and notice the best way you can behave to get what you want.

- What are the best identities that you can adopt here?

Step 8 - To finish, move away from the three positions and note down all the new possibilities for you. Is there anything you want to do differently? What do you want to do more of? What do you want to stop doing?

Notes:

Identity fraud

Identity theft is a growing problem across the globe. Criminals steal the identity of another person by using their personal details and passwords. This enables them to open bank accounts, apply for government benefits and various other fraudulent activities. In relation to this, here are a couple of interesting question to ask yourself with your goal in mind:

- Am I pretending to be someone I'm not and is this 'pretend' identity getting in my way?
- Am I committing identity fraud against myself?

If the answer to these questions is 'yes', consider changing your inner passwords to protect yourself and be true to how you really are. What are the words or phrases that you've been saying to yourself that have allowed you to be duped into thinking you're something you're not in an unhelpful way. What new words and phrases are you going to use so that you gain access to the best parts of you?

Identity and marketing yourself

In business and product marketing, identity is made up of the following:

- Logo
- Packaging
- Clothing
- Messages & Communication
- Anything visual that represents the business.

To demonstrate your strong identity in relation to your goal, everything you do should reflect this list – directly or indirectly and in real terms or metaphorically. Now that you are clear about who you are, how are you going to demonstrate your identity to others?

The clearer you become about who you are as an individual in the context of your goal or dream, the more naturally you will stand out with charisma and draw the support of others.

'The destiny of the world is determined less by the battles that are lost and won than by the stories it loves and believes in.'

Harold Goddard

Chapter SIX

VISION
S is for Stories

'Stories have power. They delight, enchant, touch, teach, recall, inspire, motivate, challenge. They help us understand.
They imprint a picture on our minds.
Consequently, stories often pack more punch than sermons. Want to make a point or raise an issue? Tell a story.'

Janet Litherland

VISION – S is for Stories

Over the past years you will have been in situations that have moulded and shaped your goals. These situations will have also confirmed your values and given you a stronger sense of what the most important things are for you.

You have taken the first two steps in developing your vision. You know what is important (your values) and you have a clear identity that supports your goal. In this chapter you will look to your past experiences for the evidence that supports your goal and then you will develop your stories about these experiences. You will take away stories to other people in detail, with passion and with purpose.

Your stories will be inspired by real situations that you have been involved in. Your memories of these situations will be the starting point. All you need for writing stories is within you right now, stored in your memory bank.

In this chapter I am giving you the **DESERT** and **PEOPLE** story-telling systems. Powerful and persuasive stories will change the state of others around you, change your own state and also embed useful beliefs.

DESERT is the first acronym for you to work with in this chapter because the metaphor is powerful and simple. Your story will be quick to construct and easy to remember.

The second activity uses the PEOPLE acronym in order to develop a more detailed story for you to use.

Effective stories engage with hearts as well as minds and one of the most common keys to our heart is other people – friends, family and others for whom we have affection and respect. Maybe you want to make a positive difference to the lives of these people as you interact and build relationships with them. As a teacher, some of the most powerful stories you can tell are about your pupils. As a health professional you might tell stories about your patients. As a leader in an organisation stories about your colleagues, team or customers might have greatest impact.

'When I was a teacher, I loved taking young people out of the classroom on fieldtrips and other outdoor education experiences. Seeing a group of bedraggled teenagers at the end of a wet and muddy walk over the moors, chatting and with big smiles on their faces, is very rewarding. The more I took groups out into the countryside, the more I realised how important such experiences were for both myself and the youngsters, despite the late nights, early mornings and being on duty for 24 hours a day. The hard work of planning and preparation felt worthwhile and the rewards and benefits gained meant that I was prepared to fight to keep such experiences in the curriculum. This was increasingly difficult due to cost, health and safety and conflicting demands on curriculum time. I can remember being in the head teacher's office one day, with the sole intention of persuading him to let me explore the possibility of an expedition to the rainforests of Brazil, using a specialist youth travel company.

The headteacher was thirty years older than me and struck an imposing figure behind his leather-topped desk. I can remember my wobbly knees and dry mouth that signified my nervousness and my words seemed to tumble out in a disorganised mess. I was in a hurry to present my case and convince him of my ability to take charge of large scale trip. One minute I felt confident and in control, as I listed out loud the wide ranging benefits to young people of taking part in previous school trips. Then I would remember what it was like to visit the head teacher's office for less positive reasons and would begin to feel intimidated and out of my depth. There were many potential barriers in my way to making an overseas project work. After the ups and downs of our discussion I can vividly remember the elation I felt having gained his permission to invite the travel company into school and take the first step of presenting the expedition to the teachers who were likely to be involved. This story always reminds me that if you don't ask, you'll never know whether or not you can have what you want. Looking back, it seemed at the time as if I was making a futile request that was bound to be turned down on the basis of my limited experience. It just goes to show that it is always worth asking.'

– Ben

A large part of Ben's success in the situation above was due to the stories he was able to tell during his discussion with the headteacher. Stories that demonstrated benefits and advantages. Stories about what young people achieved and learnt, the growth in their confidence and self esteem, barriers overcome, exam and coursework results achieved and the expanded team spirit.

Your stories will help you to persuade and influence others. You need other people to support you and maybe even help you in a practical way with time, energy or money. Stories will provide evidence that you are doing the right thing for yourself and maybe for others too. It's a bit like getting on a rollercoaster at a theme park for the first time. The people you are with are telling you about their past experiences (stories) on roller coasters; that they have been safe, it was exhilarating, and the thrill was amazing and so on. Hopefully they haven't told you stories about people being stranded upside down for several hours on roller coasters that have broken down, resulting in being rescued by fire-fighters! What do you need to know in their stories to be convinced that joining them on the rollercoaster is the right thing to do?

What do you need to know from your own personal stories that your goal and vision for the future is the right thing to embark on? That the journey with be worth it? What are your stories and how will you use them to support the development and achievement of your goal?

The DESERT story telling system

Motivation to achieve your goal comes from a thirst. Imagine your goal as an oasis in the desert. This is a fantastic metaphor to have in mind. You already have the thirst and can see the oasis ahead, but what about other people – do they?

Firstly, create a thirst in you supporters, followers or more importantly, those that aren't either of these yet, but you need them to be. Secondly, show them that the oasis (your goal) isn't a shimmering mirage – it really does exist out there in real life. Convince them that when they embark on the journey with you, they will reach a definite end point that is worthwhile and real. A desert is a place that can be barren and inhospitable, with hardships and challenges. The oasis in the distance will keep you going.

I watched Laurence of Arabia recently (an epic film from 1962 and winner of seven Academy awards, four British Academy Film Awards and five Golden Globe Awards) and the whole adventure looked so uncomfortable in the heat and dust that it definitely put me off riding camels and venturing across the desert as a 'must do' experience! Maybe this is how your family, friends or colleagues are feeling about your vision – apprehensive about the potential journey ahead and wondering if it will be worth the aggravation. Will there even be a reward at the end or are you fooling them?

Firstly, are you sure the oasis is really there, or is it just a mirage? Chapter two has taken you through the process of making your goal sure and certain. You have given it shape and colour and feeling so that it is intense and real for you. You will now be able to describe your goal in a way that is intense and real for others.

Secondly, how are you going to convince yourself and others that the journey to the oasis is going to be worth it? What do you want others to know and remember so that they will follow you to your future vision and give you their support, encouragement, time, energy and maybe even money? How will your stories provide this motivation and certainty for yourself and others? What is the danger of staying where you are? Make others thirsty for your goal with the stories you tell them and the evidence you present.

DESERT story telling system – a summary

Definite - Give them security - let your audience know that the event really did happen. They have security in knowing that you are being truthful.

Extremes - Pain and pleasure - the pleasure of achieving the outcome will be more intense if the pain was great. The bigger the gap you can create between pain and pleasure, the stronger the need to move forward away from the pain and the end point will seem even more worthwhile.

Special and strong - Does your story have clear significance for you in the way that you tell it? Does your story demonstrate strength of some sort – maybe a strong feeling that is useful or perhaps a skill or ability that you have which is a strength?

Empowerment - What did this situation enable or allow you to do? In what way did you gain more freedom or become more in control of your own direction and destiny?

Relationships - What connections did you make with people in your story? As a result of the story situation, were any existing relationships strengthened or new connections made?

Team work - Contribution - how did other people in your story support you and what did they give you? This will act as a call to action for your current friends, family or colleagues. They will see how people have helped you before and therefore what role they could or should play in the future.

Activity 1 – Using the DESERT storytelling system

Step 1 - Think of your first story right now. The story will relate to your goal in some way. It can be either:

- An experience or event that you have been involved in - something real to you that is clear in your memory, or;

- an experience or event relating to someone else, such as a historical character, a sports person, a politician, an inventor or someone else that provides the message you want or need.

Your chosen story will have informed your goal in some way. The story will be one you can tell to other people and you will be clear about it in your own mind. Your story must be about a moment in time rather than a tale spanning time. For example, instead of writing about a wonderful holiday you had for a week, choose one moment in that holiday that has the most powerful message. The case study later in this chapter will help you. Write a few words to summarise your first story in the space below:

Activity 1a

State your goal again here. I want…

_____

_____

_____

My first story that relates to my goal is…

_____

_____

_____

Activity 1b

Now use **DESERT** as a checklist. Assess whether you have included all of these elements in your story. Are any additions needed? Add brief comments or notes against each element. Refer back to the descriptors on page 115 to help you.

Definite

_____

_____

Extremes

_____

_____

Special and strong

_____

_____

Empowerment

_____

_____

Relationship

_____

_____

Team work

_____

_____

Now write your story down again (a new draft) in a format that is most practical and accessible for you. You can choose how long it needs to be so that it suits you best. Everyone is different in this respect. The longer it is, the less you are likely to remember it and the more likely you are to lose the attention of others. Here are some tips:

- Word process your story for easy editing.

- Create your story in full and keep it safe – you are less likely to use the detailed version, although it is useful to have it for reference.

- It is your story, so trust the fact that the detail will come to mind easily. It is enough to write down just the outline as this will prompt the detail to emerge from your memory.

- Have a short version of your story for everyday use that is no more than 500 words.

- Resist the temptation to learn your story word for word – you will sound less natural.

- Map your story visually, using key words, pictures, colours and symbols.

- Find a photo or object that will remind you of your story and place it somewhere visible to you as a reminder (visual anchor) of why your goal is important.

- Practise telling your story out loud and seek feedback.

Refining your stories using PEOPLE

The PEOPLE system is an alternative story telling structure. It will add more detail to your story as the system is complex. You will be able to work with the same story that you have used already in this chapter, or choose a different one if you prefer.

PEOPLE - **Step 1** - Personalities

Describe the people in your story and their characters. For each person who has a role in your story, you need to write down what they looked like, how they talked, what they were wearing, idiosyncrasies, personality traits and anything else that will bring them alive or make them stand out in a memorable way. Describe yourself at that moment in time.

P**E**OPLE - **Step 2** - Event

Describe the event (s) or the focus for this particular story. Go back to your memory of this event. Where are you? What are you doing? What happens? What are the sounds around you? What does the event look like and how does it make you feel? What is special about this event that is worth paying attention to? Paint the picture and set the scene.

PE**O**PLE - **Step 3** - Opportunities

Describe the opportunity(s) that the event presented. Maybe you learnt something or had a new experience? At the time, you might not have realised there was an opportunity for you to do something or learn something, but looking back that has now become clear.

PEO**P**LE - **Step 4** - Performance

This is about the results achieved. You might have performed in some way that demonstrated success or excellence. Somebody else who was present at the time may have achieved something relevant to your goal or that inspired you. It can also be the opposite, in that you might have failed or demonstrated poor performance in some way. Sometimes experiencing failure, loss or pain can be a stronger learning experience than success. What is the point being made by the results achieved or not achieved? Something must happen from which you can learn and develop. What did you learn? What will you avoid? What was the challenge? What was the success?

PEOPLE - **Step 5** - Lows and highs

An interesting story has a rollercoaster pattern. There are peaks and troughs of emotion, high points and low points. The best stories start with a struggle, conflict, challenge or failure and then overcome this to find a solution or take away important learning – something that can be used positively to reinforce the power, depth and importance of your vision.

PEOPLE - **Step 6** - Evidence and experience

What was the revelation from your story that supports your current goal and vision for the future? What evidence have you gathered from the story that tells you and other people that your goal and vision is the right and best way forward? You might have some statistical or empirical data (quantitative evidence) or a feeling / emotion (qualitative evidence). What is the overall experience that you gained - this could be new skills as well as new learning about yourself and others?

The last step in refining your story is to make a statement based on your evidence and experience, a bit like the motivational quotes that are scattered through this book. For example, 'As a result of this story I know that I mustn't settle for something average and it is worth taking the risk of doing something new.'

Read the first and second version of Terry's story below. Can you see which parts of the PEOPLE system are missing in version one and clearly evident in version two?

Case Study – Terry's story

Version 1 – The first paragraph – The beginning of a tale spanning decades

My father was a short, quietly spoken man with freckles, long thick brown curly hair and even thicker glasses, his stature was slight and athletic, though he was quiet he had a 'presence' which could be described as menacing. In 1974 he made the hard decision to leave Glasgow and hitchhike to London, to change and better his life. This was a difficult and heartbreaking decision for him, to leave behind his brothers and especially his sister who looked after him. He arrived in Acton, London, where he met my mother and a relationship developed, this attracted a lot of anger and upset from my mother's family and friends, I was born in May of the next year.

Version 2 – The first paragraph after it was re-drafted to show one moment in time

I entered the house with an overly excited edge, ready to explode and unleash the adventures that me and my little sister had experienced that day. However, when we entered the door of my Grandparents' house, a house of love, laughter and joy – the atmosphere was far from that. It was sombre, grey and sad. My Grandma handed me a tea towel and gestured towards the kitchen. Though no words were exchanged, I knew that my life had, in that split second, changed forever.

Which of these versions captured your imagination the most and why?

_____

_____

_____

Which of these versions did you associate with the most, as if you were really there? Why?

_____

_____

_____

The first draft of Terry's story was much too long in terms of the period of time it covered and the written length (depth of information and detail). In this form it was almost impossible for Terry to remember the story quickly and it wasn't possible to tell it to another person in just a minute or two. Use the following pages to develop your own story using the PEOPLE system. Before you begin, remember to choose just one moment in time rather than a period spanning a few days, weeks or longer.

Activity 2 – Using the PEOPLE story telling system

Step 1 - Re- state your goal here. I want…

_____

_____

_____

Step 2 - Now apply the PEOPLE system to your story so that you re-live it and enable others to re-live it with you. I have given you one page for each of the stages so that you can make lots of notes on each page as you gather your ideas together. To start with, just make notes or map out your ideas. If you prefer, you can write in full sentences. Choose whatever style suits you best, bearing in mind that for the time being, you are simply gathering and capturing ideas rather than writing the story in full.

PEOPLE - Step 1 - Personalities - the characters

- Who are the people in your story?

- What do they look like, how do they talk, what they were wearing?

- What are their personality traits? How do they make you feel?

- What else brings them alive or makes them stand out?

Notes:

PEOPLE - **Step 2** - **Event**

- What is the event?

- Where are you? What are you doing?

- What are the sounds around you?

- What does the event look like?

- How does it make you feel?

Notes:

PE**O**PLE - **Step 3** - **Opportunities**

- What was the challenge or dilemma?

- What did you learn about yourself?

- What else did you learn?

- What new things did you try?

- What is now clear to you?

Notes:

PEOPLE - **Step 4** - **Performance**

- What was the success that you could see?

- What did you achieve and how did this make you feel?

- What will you avoid?

Notes:

PEOPLE - **Step 5 - Lows and highs**

- A rollercoaster pattern.

- Peaks and troughs of emotion.

- High points and low points.

- Struggle, conflict, challenge or failure.

- Find a solution.

- Take away important learning from the story.

Notes:

PEOPLE - Step 6 - Evidence and experience

- What was the revelation?

- What evidence have you gathered?

- Empirical data (quantitative evidence).

- Feeling / emotion (qualitative evidence).

Notes:

Make a statement based on your story, a bit like the motivational quotes that are scattered through this book. For example, as a result of this story I know that *'I mustn't settle for something average and it is worth taking the risk of doing something new.'*

The motivational statement related to my story is:

_____

_____

_____

Repeat the exercises in this chapter as many times as you like. Strengthen your first story or create additional stories by choosing different experiences from your past. When you are ready, you might find it useful to write a final version of your story that can be kept somewhere for easy reference.

'All successful people are big dreamers. They imagine what their future could be, ideal in every respect, and then they work every day toward their distant vision, that goal or purpose.'

Brian Tracy

Chapter SEVEN

VISION
I is for Images

'At the end of your days do not be the kind of person who says 'I wish I had, I wish I had, I wish I had'.

Be the kind of person who says 'I'm glad I did, I'm glad I did, I'm glad I did'.'

Zig Ziglar

VISION – I is for Images

In chapter two you began to develop what you wanted to see (V), hear (A) and feel (K). The fourth step in the VISION system will focus specifically on the pictures (V) in your mind of achieving the goal. As you think about getting what you want and the steps along the way, you will engage in a three way relationship between your imagination, being inspired and creating and fine tuning the images. These images will guide you in creating the reality that you want. When you have got them just as you want them to be in your mind, you will then be able to clearly communicate them to others.

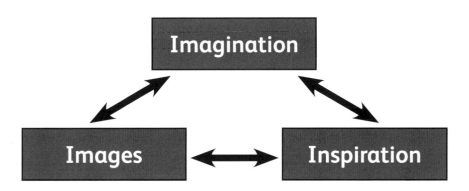

Most people use all three senses (VAK) to remember events in their lives and imagine the future. Visual representation is the most powerful sense, whereas the auditory and kinaesthetic are much more variable in their usefulness.

Visionary people can clearly see their VISION. Not only can they see it themselves, but they are able to paint the picture for other people.

Imagination, Inspiration, Images

There is a three way relationship between these elements, each as important as the others. It is possible to move freely between these three elements in any order. For best results, all three elements should be present in your goal. Activity 1 provides you with some questions to guide your initial thinking for these three elements. You may like to make notes as you read this section and space has been provided for this. You may find the same ideas are repeated several times as you consider the questions or you may answer each question differently. Both approaches are fine.

Activity 1 – Imagination, Inspiration, Images

State your goal here. I want…

_____

_____

_____

What can you **see** when you imagine achieving what you want?

_____

_____

_____

_____

What new **images** can you create in your imagination?

_____

_____

_____

_____

What can you imagine when you **see** yourself and others achieving?

_____

_____

_____

_____

What is the **picture** of the perfect end point?

_____

_____

_____

_____

In your mind's eye, **see** the memories for the past – events, situations, people or maybe something else that has inspired your vision. I can see…

_____

_____

_____

_____

What can you suddenly create when you put your mind to it?

_____

_____

_____

_____

What are the pictures that will breathe life into (inspire) your vision? I can see…

_____

_____

_____

_____

What have you **seen** before that will help you – what are the pictures in your mind from previous experiences that will inspire and inform your vision? I can see…

_____

_____

_____

_____

What are the **images** of the end point – what **pictures** will tell you that your VISION has been achieved? I can see…

_____

_____

_____

_____

How can you work even better with these elements to create your best images of the future? In the rest of this chapter you will work through three activities – the Disney Strategy, a vision board and a guided visualisation script.

The Disney Strategy

The Disney Strategy is simple and effective. Thinking about Disney might make you smile as there could be positive associations for you, such as watching Disney movies or visiting one of the theme parks.

The Disney strategy is split into three phases, and the first one is relevant to this chapter. Phases 2 and 3 are relevant to the next chapter and you will work with them later in the book.

The Disney Strategy was created by Robert Dilts and is described in detail in his book 'Strategies of Genius Volume 1'. Through creating the Disney Strategy, Dilts has simplified Walt Disney's amazing ability for 'Imagineering'. Disney took his imagined vision for films and themes parks and made them real – just like you are going to do. The Disney Strategy has three phases.

1. **Dreamer phase** - Here there is an attitude of anything is possible and nothing is impossible – modern phrases to describe this are 'blue sky thinking' or 'thinking out of the box'.

2. **Realist phase** - The plan of action to make the dream come true and the steps you will take. This will be covered in the next chapter

3. **Critic phase** - Distance yourself from your ideas and apply logic and analysis. Problems, pitfalls, risks and shortcomings can all be discussed in this stage and will be included in the next chapter.

The beauty of the Disney Strategy is that it forces you to pay equal attention to all aspects of having an idea. As human beings we have different preferences in our approach to the future and I am sure you can think of people that you know who would more naturally fit into the Critic phase rather than the Dreamer phase for example. My natural preference and area of comfort is the Dreamer phase, and as a result my risk management strategies and attention to detail can sometimes let me down. Working alongside a person who is more naturally a Critic is good for me as it takes me out of my comfort zone and gives a more rounded approach. The Disney strategy is a great structure for ensuring that all aspects of your creative approach have been covered.

> *'All our dreams can come true – if we have the courage to pursue them.'* Walt Disney

Activity 2 – Getting started – the Dreamer phase

The Dreamer is the person for whom all things are possible and this phase generates alternatives and possibilities. In this phase you will think about the big picture. Any idea is a good idea, no matter how big, small or whacky it might be. In this stage, ban yourself from making any judgements about your ideas. The assumption is that all of your ideas are perfect. 'Disney the dreamer was visionary, saw the big picture and believed in what was possible' (Dilts).

There are some questions on the next few pages to prompt you in generating ideas in the dreaming state. This activity is split into two clear steps.

Step 1 - Now think about the end point (the goal) and all the possibilities for how it might look. Use the questions on the next page to prompt you. Write all your ideas in the space provided. At this stage, just write about what you (or other people) will see when you have achieved this. Avoid general statements about vague ideas and instead, describe reaching your goal in pictures. A helpful way of looking at this task is to imagine taking a photo of the final goal and describe what you will see in the photo. Remember to include all the ideas that come to mind, no matter how simple, complicated or ambitious they seem – no judgement or criticism is allowed – just capture everything and avoid saying things like this:

- It won't work.

- I've already tried that.

- It will cost too much.

- I don't have time.

- Other people won't like it.

- That's all very well, but...

	The end point – how the goal might look when I've achieved it
What ideas do I see?	I will see...
What even better ideas do I see?	
What other possibilities can I see?	

	The end point – how the goal might look when I've achieved it
What do I want to see myself achieving?	I will have achieved…
What are the payoffs?	
How do I see myself celebrating?	

Step 2 – Dreaming about the steps you could take to get to your goal. This includes all the possible activities you could be involved in and all the ideas for actions you could take. Assume that all ideas are good ideas. Think about all the things you could be doing to achieve what you want. Imagine there are no restrictions. Time and money are no object. If you were a fly on the wall watching yourself doing things to get to where you want to be, what could you be doing?

Write your ideas in the space provided.

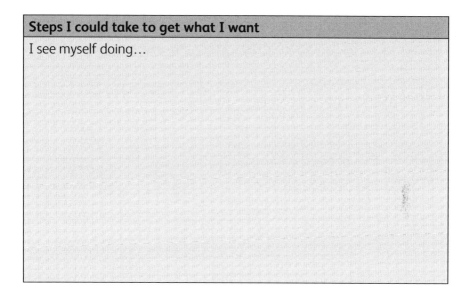

Steps I could take to get what I want
I see myself doing…

OK, great, so now that you have used your imagination and been inspired, let's fine-tune your images.

Creating a vision board

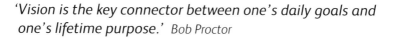

> '*Vision is the key connector between one's daily goals and one's lifetime purpose.*' Bob Proctor

Vision boards are a popular way to support you in visualising your goal and they are designed to use the power of the law of attraction. The law of attraction (Hill 1928 and Wattles 1910) assumes that what enters your life is a result of what you attract into your life. By building a mental picture of what you want, you will attract positive ways to make it happen.

Activity 3 – Your vision board

Ingredients:

- A variety of old magazines or brochures

- Scissors and glue

- A large piece of backing card, paper or board

Assemble all your ingredients and be prepared to make a mess! The size of your vision board can be anything, from quite small (A4 is probably the smallest) to massive. Bear in mind that you will need to display it somewhere so have this in mind when you choose your backing material. Vision boards work well pinned to a cork board or stuck on a fridge with magnets, so choose something light enough to stay in place and big enough to be seen and have impact.

Create your vision board, by cutting out images relating to your goal (or pictures that are symbolic of your goal in some way) from magazines and brochures. Stick them together in a big montage that you can display somewhere prominent. Some people like to prepare by creating a word list to capture key ideas and themes before seeking images, whilst others are more inspired by starting with pictures rather than words. Both approaches are fine. You can include words, quotes or mantras in your board.

Your vision board represents things you want to have. The pictures act as a positive emotional connector for your vision. You may well have created a vision board before at home, school or work.

The reticular activating system (RAS) is the information filtering system in your brain. Vision boards work by programming the RAS to tune into things in your environment that can help you move closer towards your goal. The RAS tags information that is important to you, stores it within your neurology and then pays attention to it in your environment. An example of this is when a new parent has been programmed to tune in to the small snuffles or whimpers of their baby at night, yet they sleep soundly as a severe storm passes by. Maybe you've bought a new coat and all of a sudden you notice other people wearing the same or similar coat. By programming your RAS with a vision board, the theory is that your RAS will seek out things in your environment that are aligned with it, which is the same principle as the Law of Attraction.

Figure 14: Sally and Terry's VISION boards

Tristan Loo suggests that the following four factors are all important for the best vision boards:

- **Visual stimulation** – plenty of pictures, words and phrases to stimulate your mind.

- **Emotional content** – your pictures should evoke a positive emotional response and fuel your passion to achieve your goal.

- **Strategically-placed** – a location that gives you maximum exposure for the law of attraction to work best.

- **Personal confidence in displaying your board** – if you fear criticism or justification of your vision board from others, then place it in a private location – negative feelings, self-doubt, and criticism can sabotage the potential impact of your vision board.

The longer you take with your vision board the better. There may be a temptation to rush this activity as it can be fun, quick and easily completed in under an hour. However, the more inspired and heartfelt your board is, the greater the impact it will have for you and the more transformational it will be. Your vision board should be memorable, passionate and positive. Finish with a few empowering words, slogan or a memorable phrase. Here are a few borrowed from advertising:

Nike – *Just do it!*

McDonalds – *I'm lovin' it!*

Apple – *The power to be your best*

Starburst – *Isn't life juicy*

Activity 4

Return to chapter five and take another look at your positive and resourceful 'I am…' statements. These will support you in achieving what you want. You can use these again here as affirmations for your vision board. Say them to yourself or out loud, write them somewhere memorable or post them on a sticky note where you will see them. Choose two or three of your 'I am…' statements and re-write them in the space below as affirmations.

I am…

Activity 5 – An advanced visualisation script

At the end of chapter two you completed a short visualisation exercise for your goal. Visionary people store their pictures of their goal in two very particular ways:

- There is more than one picture.

- The pictures are moving, like a film running on a screen.

To experience this yourself, repeat the guided visualisation exercise from chapter two using the more detailed script below. This new script is fine-tuned to add extra pictures and to create a movie in your mind. Refer back to chapter two if it would help to review the instructions.

Visualisation script

"Close your eyes and relax ……. Let's begin with a few slow deep breaths ……. as you let go of each breath, release any tension or stress that you may be holding on to ……. as you feel yourself relaxing notice a picture in your mind of you having achieved your goal ……. the best way is a movie in the top right hand corner as you watch it right now ……. Allow your imagination to create several moving pictures of you having achieved the goal ……. Absorb yourself in the experience ……. as if you are really there.

See achieving the goal as a movie ……. As if you are in it ……. You are watching it through your own eyes. Notice everything around you as you know you've achieved your goal. What can you see? ……. What are you doing? ……. Where are you? ……. Who else is there? ……. What else is going on? ….. What are you feeling? …..

There may be more than one movie ……. a bit like a split screen with different movies side by side ……. adjust it so it's just right for you ……. make the pictures of the movie bigger and closer to you ……. Imagine you have a remote control and turn up the intensity ……. Change the colour and the contrast ……. the brightness ……. the sounds ……. anything else that makes it more alive and a more powerful experience for you .... there may be things you want to turn down to make it better .... adjust it some more ....

If there is frame around the movie take it away so that the movie is all around you. Bring in more detail and notice the increased intensity of all the different feelings you have now your goal has been achieved.

Turn it up some more to create the experience of what it will be like when you achieve this.

What are you thinking now that you have achieved that goal?

What are you saying to yourself?

What are you saying to other people?

What are you feeling? .... Notice where that feeling is inside you .... Does it have a shape or colour? .... Is that feeling moving or still? .... Turn that feeling up some more .... that's great.

Take a little while longer to enjoy your sense of happiness, fulfilment or something else that you notice is powerful for you.

Now that you are thinking, hearing, seeing, and touching everything as you would if you were actually there, it's time to come back to now, knowing it can be as you want it to be. Leave your movie out there in the future and step out .... You can see yourself in it over there .... but you're watching yourself from a distance.

When you are ready .... knowing that the future you want is there for you .... come back to now and be aware of the room and where you are sitting .... open your eyes and come back into the present moment. Stretch and smile."

Reflection – what happens now when you think about your goal?

_____

_____

_____

_____

What else has changed?

_____

_____

_____

_____

The final step - Now that you have clear and refined pictures of your goal, check out your internal feelings. You should have a very strong sense that what you are doing is the right thing to be doing because the movie running in your mind looks and feels the strongest and best it can be. This is your final check. Your imagination and inspiration has done some great work. Everyone is different in how this feeling is represented and only you will know if that feeling is telling you to put yourself out there and get what you want. The feeling may have a particular location in your body, it may have a shape or colour or something else. Whatever it is, trust it even if you can't articulate it.

Here are some typical quotes of what people say at this stage of the process, which means they know their vision is strong:

- 'It is a palpable feeling – enhanced, growing, strong and upright – this is my test.'

- 'I know in my heart of hearts.'

- 'It is in my soul.'

- 'I am going to step up to the mark.'

- 'My head doesn't come into it as it would create problems of over analysis, measuring, ticking boxes – it is a heart and soul feeling instead.'

- 'I have a gut instinct.'

- 'I just know.'

Activity 6

To finish this chapter, use the space on the next page to write or draw a summary of your thoughts and feeling in the way that suits you best. Here are two examples:

Grey and pink suit. Staff meeting.

Pink and purple colours swirling around the picture – calming.

Feeling happy and elated.

I am going to be able to do this

Big comfy chair, smell of coffee, heard laughter, large clock and journal open on desk.

Figure 15: Catherine's visual and written summary of this chapter

'There is a warm glow that radiates from my chest – happy, comfortable, at ease.

No justification just realisation. I am rewarding everyone with a great holiday in celebration of working together and achieving the goal. I am being happy in what I am doing and not having to take it to the next level. I am doing things that are right for me and also for my family.'

Figure 16: Rob's written summary of this chapter

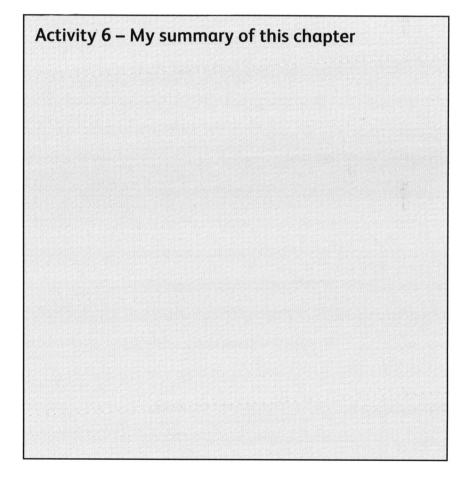

Activity 6 – My summary of this chapter

'I think we all have blocks between us
and the best version of ourselves, whether
it's shyness, insecurity, anxiety, whether it's
a physical block, and the story of a person
overcoming that block to their best self.
It's truly inspiring because I think all of us
are engaged in that every day.'

Tom Hooper

Chapter EIGHT

VISION
O is for Options

'Information can bring you choices and choices bring power - educate yourself about your options and choices. Never remain in the dark of ignorance.'

Joy Page

VISION – O is for Options

Many of the activities in this book so far have helped you develop ideas and possibilities for your goals. In chapter two you created a simple goal map, where different elements and ideas for your goal were shown in a simple visual pattern. In chapter seven you spent some time dreaming about the possibilities for what you could achieve and the steps you could take to get there. This chapter is about beginning to make choices and plans about the steps you could take and the order you might take them in. The following activities will take you back to a place of reality so that you can begin to address potential problems and start to make decisions about what to do next – in the short, medium and long term. By the end of this chapter you will have some answers to these two key questions:

- What are the realistic and practical **opportunities** that are available to me?

- What are my **options** for taking action over the next few weeks and beyond?

Firstly, let's go back to the Disney Strategy, which you started in the previous chapter by immersing yourself in the Dreamer phase. Now you will enter the phase of the Critic and the Realist. Robert Dilts stated that Walt Disney *'represents the process of turning fantasies into concrete and tangible expressions'*. By adopting different perceptual positions (the skill of noticing more points of view than your own as described on page 100), Dilts discovered that Disney was able to step out of the Dreaming position and into the shoes of the Critic and Realist.

This gave him a tangible product via the Realist and a high quality product by thinking as the Critic. You will now do the same.

The Disney Strategy links clearly with the three perceptual positions shown overleaf:

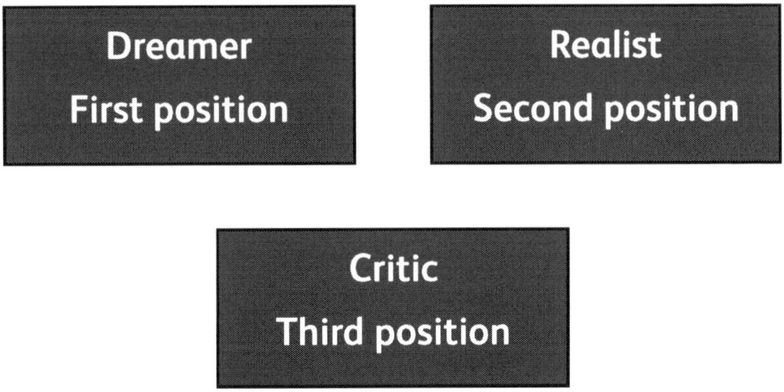

┌─────────────────────┐   ┌─────────────────────┐
│   Dreamer   │   │   Realist   │
│   First position   │   │   Second position   │
└─────────────────────┘   └─────────────────────┘

┌─────────────────────┐
│   Critic   │
│   Third position   │
└─────────────────────┘

Figure 17: The relationship between perceptual positions and the Disney Strategy

Dreamer phase – the attitude of anything is possible and nothing is impossible – modern phrases to describe this are 'blue sky thinking' or 'thinking out of the box'. This was the focus for chapter seven (Imagination, Inspiration, Images). **First position** is about you being fully involved in achieving your goal.

Realist phase – step away from your personal views to plan the smaller steps you will take. Act as if the goal is possible. **Second position** is about considering different perspectives and reactions.

Critic phase – separate yourself from the goal and examine problems, pitfalls, risks and shortcomings. Criticise the ideas or the plan, not yourself or others. **Third position** is the place where you take a detached perspective and remove personal emotions (yourself and others) to find solutions to problems.

Activity 1 will introduce you to the Realist and Critic phases and there is an opportunity to bring together all three phases (Dreamer, Realist and Critic) in one written summative exercise. Activity 2 will show you how to apply some critical and creative thinking tools to the potential problems and pitfalls of your goal (Critic phase). In the next chapter you will move on to produce an action plan and personal development plan, both of which will further support the Realist phase of the Disney Strategy.

Activity 1 – The Disney Strategy continued

The Realist is the person who sorts things out and helps to define actions and make plans. In this phase you will be practical in your thinking and evaluate the ideas you 'dreamt' of in the last chapter. You will start to think about the steps you can take and how others might be involved. As you do this, you will be in second position in the perceptual positions model. You will step away from your personal involvement in your goal and ideas and apply some rational thinking and planning without the emotional involvement of the Dreamer (first position). You may consider the views of others at this stage.

State your goal here. I want…

_____

_____

_____

Now consider the questions on the next page in relation to what you want.

The Realist

What resources do I already have? Be precise and practical.

_____

_____

_____

_____

What new resources do I need?

_____

_____

_____

_____

What is my first/next step?

_____

_____

_____

_____

What evidence or feedback will I seek to check that I am making progress?

_____

_____

_____

_____

Where will it be done?

_____

_____

_____

_____

How will it be done?

_____

_____

_____

_____

When will each step be implemented?

_____

_____

_____

_____

When will each step be completed?

_____

_____

_____

_____

In the **Critic phase** you will now act as if you are a person who picks up on the bits that don't fit. You will apply logic by standing back and seeing all points of view. This is the same as third position as you will be detached from the situation – a bit like an independent observer. You can see the big picture, you're not emotionally involved and you can notice many points of view. Here are some questions that fit well in this phase:

Who might be positively or negatively affected by the steps I could take towards my goal?

_____

_____

_____

_____

_____

_____

Under what circumstances would I not proceed?

_____

_____

_____

_____

_____

_____

Who will make or break the effectiveness of the idea - what are their needs?

_____

_____

_____

_____

_____

_____

_____

_____

When and where would I **not** want to implement my new ideas?

_____

_____

_____

_____

_____

_____

_____

Disney Strategy – A Summary – Bring all your thoughts together by recording a summary of them here. You could use a mixture of words, colour, pictures or symbols.

DREAMER – First position – your ideas and imagination with no judgement

REALIST – Second position – rational thinking – steps and procedures

CRITIC – Third position – independent observations from many points of view

Finally, when you are using the Disney Strategy, which is your naturally preferred phase? Which is most uncomfortable for you? When you have a sense of this, think about who could support you in the phases that you find most uncomfortable. If you find the critic phase most difficult, who in your life is good at asking critical questions? How could you plan to involve them or spend more time with them? Where would be the best place to meet and would you invite anyone else? Do you want them to coach you (ask you brilliantly critical questions) or mentor you (advise and guide you with their thoughts, ideas and past experience)? Who else could you talk to?

Activity 2 – Who is going to be in my team?

In the spaces below, write the names of real people in your life who could support you and help you to develop your thinking in each phase of the Disney Strategy. If you've not met or found them yet, who could it be? Where do you need to look or who do you need to ask to find the people that you need?

Dreamer – my team

Realist – my team

Critic – my team

Critical and creative thinking

Critical and creative thinking are both helpful for solving problems and for creating new opportunities out of situations that before seemed stuck. Most of us, through conditioning, upbringing and habit, rely on thinking in an analytical or critical way to generate solutions to problems or some new ideas. The characteristics of this type of thinking do not lend themselves to exploring all possible alternatives or looking at options which may appear unconventional or irrational on first appearance.

Critical thinking operates in a step by step way. It operates within boundaries. Critical thinking is logical and excludes possibilities through rational argument and therefore results in fewer solutions. It makes assumptions about what is possible. Finally, the whole approach is focused towards achieving a result. Once an argument has been reduced to the bare bones, you can go no further with this thinking style.

Creative thinking operates randomly and without structure or boundaries. It is designed to generate many alternative solutions. It explores all possibilities, whether conventional or not. Creative thinking does not attempt to limit choices and reduce findings to a single solution. Ideas are explored from many angles and alternatives expand rather than decrease.

Critical thinking is often represented as taking place in the 'left brain' and creative thinking in the 'right brain'. Roger Sperry received a Nobel Prize in 1962 for identifying these separate intellectual functions of the brain and to this day, our understanding of how this works is still very basic. Positron Emission Tomography (PET) and Magentic Resonance Imaging (MRI) scanning is now helping with scientific research in this area. One of Sperry's original studies involved working with people whose corpus callosum had been severed so that left and right brain connections no longer operated. The two side of the brain were no longer able to communicate and they performed different functions.

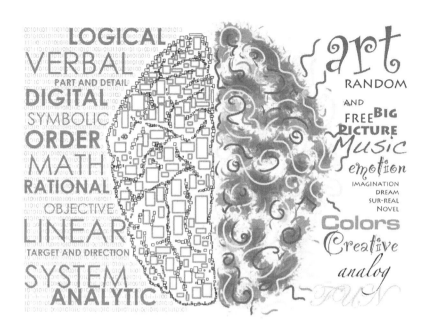

Live images of the brain operating on a screen, indicate areas that are used for specific skills and thinking. When a person is engaged in creative thinking, both the left and right brain are active and this shows that the traditional ways describing our left and right brains as critical and creative are over-simplistic.

Although each hemisphere is dominant in certain activities, they are both basically skilled in all areas, and critical as well as creative thinking skills are actually distributed throughout the cortex of the brain. An important point is that neither technique is superior to the other.

Critical thinking and creative thinking are not 'either/or' choices, and both are useful. Overleaf are some examples of thinking tools and techniques, which can be applied to generating new ideas and solving problems.

The left and the right hemispheres of the brain are connected by the corpus callosum, which is formed of nerve fibres that allow the two sides of the brain to communicate. Roger Gorski has published widely about

Critical thinking	Creative thinking
Convergent and Critical	Divergent and Creative
De Bono's Thinking Hats	Intuitive
Defining the problem	Ideas shower
Action planning	Story boards
Analysing and practical	Mind Maps
Deductive	Inductive
Step by step and linear	Exploratory
Rational argument	Adventurous & Random
Left brain – language and words	No limits and big picture
Drill down - detail	Left and right brain together
Cause & effect – Fishbone Analysis	Right brain - visualisation
Systematic reasoning	Random simulation

the differences between the male and female brain. He has discovered that women have up to 30% more connections between right and left hemispheres, and the male and female brains work differently on the same task. It is thought that up to 20% of men have feminised brains and about 10% of women have strong masculine wiring traits.

The brain is a muscle, so like any muscle, to increase its flexibility and strength it needs to be exercised so that you can expand your strategies for using it. Education and business in western society tends to favour left brain approaches, so right brain functions are normally the ones that need developing further.

The education system in which you grew up probably discouraged day dreaming and intuition, with creative subjects in schools frequently having had less status compared to more traditional academic and logical subjects (such as the sciences, history or maths). The skills that enable people to achieve academic success, go to university and succeed at work are probably left brain dominant. You have already begun to flex your right brain muscles by developing your goal map, values, identity and stories. You will learn the most from working out of your comfort zone, so persevere, even if at the time it seems awkward or strange.

The first activity that follows engages more of the left brain. The second is more creative and involves left and right working together.

Working with problems

In the next activity you will consider some of the problems you might face in relation to your goal. Some potential problems might have emerged from your earlier thinking whilst in the Critic phase of the Disney strategy. By examining the pitfalls both critically and creatively, new options and opportunities will be presented. This is a great way to move problems forward and change them from being a stuck state to a resourceful state.

Activity 3 – Getting started with problems

State your goal. I want…

_____

_____

_____

_____

_____

_____

_____

List some potential practical problems (challenges or barriers) in relation to your goal and in any order.

_____

_____

_____

Now consider which of these problems are under your control (i.e. you have influence or the option to change something). Re-write these here.

_____

_____

_____

Now choose two problems from the list above that you would like to consider for the rest of this chapter. Size doesn't matter. They might be big or small. The problems you choose must be something that you can influence or change, even if they seem big or daunting at this stage. An example of this could be the problem of not enough time, where you can't change the number of hours in a day, although you can change or influence how you use some of those hours. Highlight your choice in some way.

Now you are going to apply two different techniques that will generate thoughts and ideas to support you in making changes and doing something differently:

- fishbone analysis (critical thinking), and;

- random simulation (creative thinking).

An example of critical thinking - Fishbone Analysis (Ishikawa)

Fishbone analysis is a tool that was created by Kaoru Ishikawa in 1968 as part of his pioneering work on total quality management in the shipyards of Kawasaki in Japan. It is used for drilling down to identify root causes  of a problem. Very often problems are stated in general terms. By drilling down it can be possible to identify smaller aspects of the problem where it is easier to take action or find solutions. By solving a small part there can be positive knock on effect onto other aspects of the problem, therefore reducing the scale of the problem or solving it completely, and thereby keeping forward progress and momentum.

On the next page is an example of a completed fish bone analysis so that you have an idea of what you are aiming to produce. The focus for Ashley's fishbone is privatisation at work, which initially seemed to be a problem that was out of his control. However by drilling down, there emerged some practical options and steps that wouldn't change the event of privatisation itself, but would change how Ashley reacted and responded to the event in a more resourceful way. Terry chose to focus on new strategies regarding money. Later on in this chapter you will find out how the random simulation activity added to Ashley's thinking about how to best mange impending privatisation of the organisation that he works for.

Activity 4 – Fishbone Analysis

You need some plain paper and a pen. Use Ashley's example on the next page and Sally's example on page 170 to help you with the appearance of your fishbone and also to stimulate your ideas.

1. Turn your paper to landscape. Write down a problem that you have identified on one far side of the paper where the head of the fish might be (summarise the problem with one or two words) and then draw a line for the backbone of the fish.

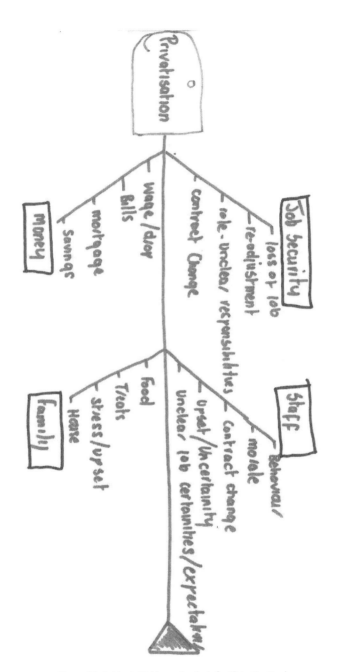

Figure 18: Ashley's Fishbone Analysis for 'Privatisation'

2. Think about the main areas that are contributing to the problem. Between 6 and 8 are manageable at this stage. Draw lines (fish bones) going from the spine for each factor.

3. For each of the factors, think about the causes. Draw these as smaller lines coming from your fish bones.

Fish Bone analysis – Reflections

Analyse the finished diagram by looking at the smallest factors that are contributing to the overall problem. If you were to choose one small area to solve first, what would it be?

_____

_____

_____

_____

What would be the positive knock on effect of this?

_____

_____

_____

_____

What are your next steps going to be?

_____

_____

_____

_____

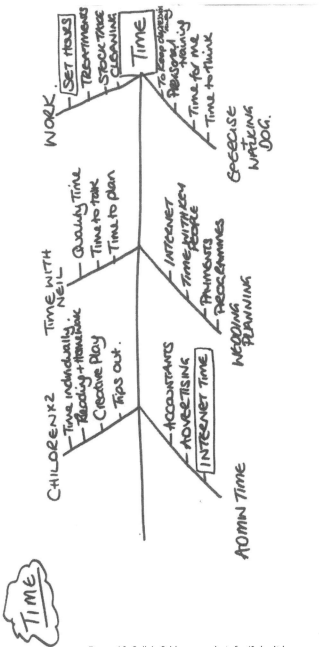

Figure 19: Sally's fishbone analysis for 'I don't have enough time'

Activity 5 – Random simulation

This is an example of creative thinking. Random simulation is used extensively in marketing for generating original ideas for promotional campaigns, especially if the process has got stuck or is lacking imagination.

You will need a dictionary (any type or size) and somewhere else to write all the ideas and solutions that will be generated by this exercise.

This is a great tool for generating additional and sometimes unexpected solutions or ideas. It may seem a bit of a random approach (excuse the pun!), but it really does work. The dictionary is the basis for selecting random words and creating new associations and ideas.

Choose any problem related to your goal and summarise it here

_____

_____

_____

Step 1 - If your dictionary has 500 pages, create a list of seven random numbers from 0 to 500. Adapt this according to the size of your dictionary. You will be using these as page numbers later in the exercise. Write down the number of pages in your dictionary and then write your random numbers.

There are _____ dictionary pages in total.

Number list 1: (0 - 500)

_____

Now create a list of 7 random numbers from 1 to 10. You can use the same number more than once. You will be using these to select random words from the dictionary.

Number list 2: (1 - 10)

_____

Step 2 - Now the fun begins. Take your dictionary and select the first number from number list 1. Turn to this page in your dictionary. For example, if your first random number on your first list is 250, turn to page 250 in your dictionary. Now use your second list of number numbers from 1 to 10 to select a word on that page. If you choose number 6, go to the 6th key word in the page. Write this word down in the space below and if it helps, write a short version of the definition too. Repeat (stick to the rules of the exercise) until you have at least seven words written down in the gaps below. This is your random word list and be prepared for some unusual or surprising words.

Word 1 _____

Word 2 _____

Word 3 _____

Word 4 _____

Word 5 _____

Word 6 _____

Word 7 _____

Step 3 - Spend some time to generate ideas to solve your problem by forcing an association between the first word and the problem. The link isn't supposed to be natural – that's the whole point of the activity so you can still be confident if it seems uncomfortable or weird! Before you begin, three finished examples of this activity follow, to help you with this step. The dictionary words for each person have been listed, with a brief summary of their associations between the word and the problem.

Case Study 1 – Ashley – The problem was privatisation at work

Goal statement: 'I want to cope successfully with privatisation of my organisation and possible redundancy.'

Random word list and associations

1. **Afterbirth** – empty womb – I must ensure I am free of all debts.

2. **Comedy** – to worry less and laugh more.

3. **Consecutive** – unfaltering – a bit like a saving scheme – ensure I save the same amount each month.

4. **Hornblende** – dark brown, black or green mineral – colours remind me of bank notes – pay attention to money.

5. **Madrigal** – a song for several unaccompanied voices –allow other people to help me in my outcome.

6. **Slack** – wage drop – prepare for this – it doesn't matter as much as I thought.

"I have a problem looming over me which is the potential for my organisation to be privatised sometime soon and therefore my job or terms of employment might be at risk. The fishbone analysis brought to my attention that I am worried about money, and I hadn't really noticed that before. I felt like privatisation was being 'done to me' and although I can't change the situation, I now know that I can easily do new things to manage it better. The random words have highlighted some new strategies for saving money that I hadn't previously considered. My first word from the dictionary was 'afterbirth' and my initial reaction was 'yuk'. A few seconds later I had a better image in my mind of an empty womb after the birth of a baby and for me this represented being debt free. I felt surprisingly elated by this and I started to write down ways that I could achieve being debt free and made a commitment to myself to open a new savings account at the bank. This was a completely new idea for me".

Case Study 2 – Sally – The problem was not enough time for work activity

Goal statement: 'To make my business successful enough to pay me a wage of £20,000 per year'

"My first word from the dictionary exercise was acidulous, which means 'slightly acid'. I know that my personal approach to people and situations can be negative and this word prompted me to think that maybe I'm not being approachable and that might stop me from getting business and therefore reduce my income and potential capital. To change this I want to be more like the second word on my list, which is 'canary'. A yellow song bird, which in my mind is more approachable, relaxed and has a sunny disposition. There is a singing aspect in how I can talk about my business with others in a way that generates new business. My third word was the noun 'clip', which is an object for holding things together. From this I want to focus more on making links between myself and the bank so that we have a stronger relationship. The more I stay in touch with the bank and make visits to my branch, the more likely they are to understand my business and therefore lend me money."

I will now look at time positively and manage it differently to how I did before. I will stop saying 'I've not got enough time'. I can make time."

Case Study 3 – Chris – The problem was not knowing when to give up part time work and focus on a new business opportunity

Random word list and associations

1. **Classic** – move away from 'classic' way of earning income which is exchanging time for £'s.

2. **Flimsy** – clients can currently cancel at any time in my part time work, which isn't great for business.

3. **Prefix** – alters meaning of the word work.

4. **Akimbo** – be open and welcoming to new streams of income.

5. **Countermand** – means cancel an order – I could save £100 per year by cancelling insurance that I don't need any more.

6. **Seedy** – the seeds are planted – go reap the harvest.

7. **Astray** – without my previous role my mind / energy will be more focussed on the new business venture. There will be less wandering mentally and physically, which is good because this causes me to go astray from my new business goal.

Step 3 continued - Just like these examples, you might have quite a lot to write into order to create the link between the word and your goal. A few words or a short sentence might be enough, depending on your thinking style. You could also create lots of options and links for each word. In the following spaces, write your goal statement and then re-write your random words. For each one, create an association with your goal and note down new ideas or solutions that come to mind.

My Goal is...

_____

_____

_____

Word 1 _____

_____

_____

_____

_____

Word 2 _____

_____

_____

_____

_____

Word 3 _____

_____

_____

_____

_____

_____

Word 4 _____

_____

_____

_____

_____

Word 5 _____

_____

_____

_____

_____

_____

Word 6 _____

_____

_____

_____

_____

Word 7 _____

_____

_____

_____

_____

Summary

We have preferences for how we prefer to think about our goals and problems. Maybe you are most comfortable generating new ideas, whilst others around you find this overwhelming and lacking in detail and substance. Alternatively, you may be very good at managing risks and putting in pace detailed steps, but feel uncomfortable with grand plans and vague ideas. Here are some of the pitfalls of always working in your comfort zone:

- You might miss new opportunities and options.

- You might achieve what you want more slowly than you anticipated.

- Unforeseen problems might occur in higher numbers, draining your time and energy.

- You might be less balanced in your approach to working with goals and therefore less effective in achieving them.

- You may not gain the support of people around you who work in a different way to you.

- Your ideas may stagnate or fall apart if the day to day steps haven't been considered.

To reduce the likelihood of pitfalls on this list becoming true for you, consider the following:

- Find yourself a professional coach who will challenge you to think out of your comfort zone, encourage you in your least preferred ways of thinking and create balance in your approach.

- Create a team of people around you who can have the attributes and working styles that you find more uncomfortable. If you are at home drilling down into the detail and plans of the Realist phase or the useful pessimism of the Critic phase, find others who can support and energise you in generating ideas.

- Put time aside in your diary to engage with a specific tool or technique from this book that you wouldn't naturally choose.

- Research and use other tools and techniques for critical and creative thinking.

- Create balance by preparing ahead – before you spend some time working on your goals (by yourself, with a team or someone else) prepare templates for tools or activities that will support you in thinking creatively and critically, rather than relying on your default setting.

Now you are ready to collate all of your ideas for what to do next. Successful visionary people don't just have a clear sense of the goal; they also have a free flow of ideas for practical steps they can take to make things happen. These ideas need to be captured and written down, so now is the time to find a notebook or create a folder in your computer where you can literally 'dump' your ideas and possible steps in a place where they can be kept safe. Ready for when you need them.

This chapter has presented some tools and techniques for consciously thinking about ideas, options and problems. You will continue to have many, many more creative ideas over the next few days, weeks and months and it is highly probable that you already had ideas and possibilities for what to do next before you began reading this book. The key to success with your vision is recording your thoughts before they are lost and then putting in place a plan.

As you start talking to people about your vision, new ideas will come to mind and other people will also have great suggestions for helping you to achieve what you want. These all need to be written down as soon as possible so they can be remembered, referred to and picked up when you are ready. Many people choose to buy a special notebook just for this purpose. A small one is perfect as you can carry it around with you more easily. Another option is to purchase a voice capture device or use similar software on your phone, as often the best ideas come to us when we are relaxed, away from work, driving or engaging in a leisure activity. Keep a notebook or device handy in different places, such as your car, the kitchen, your work bag or in the pocket of your favourite coat.

As Henry Ford famously said, "If you do what you've always done, you'll get what you've always got." What new options and opportunities are waiting for you?

'Ideas can be life changing. Sometimes all you need to open the door is just one more good idea.'

Jim Rohn

Chapter NINE

VISION
N is for Next Steps

'Dream big, but allow yourself the opportunity to start small, and have your share of struggles in the beginning. The world's greatest composers weren't writing symphonies the day they first sat at a piano.'

Kevin O'Rourke

VISION – N is for Next Steps

Now that you have lots of ideas and options, it's time to formulate your next steps. You need a way that is tangible and concrete and empowers you to move forward against a timetable. This is the stage at which you will probably want to start talking to other people about your vision and get them involved in supporting or helping you. It is important that you are clear about some of the practical steps you can start to take. Some of these steps you will undertake yourself and sometimes you will want (or need) to enlist the support of others. For example, you might choose to delegate activities or areas of responsibility to a person or team that has skills that you don't currently have.

Delegation is essential if you want to accelerate the rate at which you achieve your vision. You have limited time and energy and therefore if you aim to undertake all the steps on your own, you are putting a limit on the speed at which you achieve what you want. This might not matter, although most people don't want to limit their level of success. Why would you?

Another major benefit of delegating tasks and responsibilities is that it will reduce your workload and therefore lessen the potential for pressure and stress. This chapter will take you through some tools for being able to explain your strategy (the steps) for achieving your vision to other people so that you complete the right task with the right person at the right time. This is better than creating your plan in a hit and miss way as you go.

Aims and Objectives

Before you involve other people, you will need to be clear in your own mind about aims and objectives for your vision. This will provide a short summary that is clear and concise that you can then use as the basis for a written or verbal summary of your plan.

Aims can be described as a broad statement of what you want and your intentions. You have been used to working with the statement of your goal throughout this book and this will form the basis for stating your aims. If it helps at this stage, consider the goal and the aims to be the same thing. Aims paint a brief picture of what you are seeking to achieve and shouldn't include any reference to the steps or 'how' you are going to achieve it. You should create two or three statements about your aims.

Objectives are the steps you are going to take and in the previous chapter you will have come up with lots of different ideas for possible steps. At this stage you don't need to state every step. Instead, choose a small number of very feasible and clear tasks that you are committed to in the near future. The objectives should address the most pressing steps or tasks that you want to complete. Your objectives will be sensible and precise so that they state exactly what you will be doing first.

At this stage you are considering the aims and objectives at a wide level (the big picture). You are saying to the world 'This is what I want to achieve and these are the first steps towards achieving it.' How you might use the aims and objectives depends upon the context for your vision. Here are some situations where being clear about your aims and objectives could be important:

Enlisting the informal support of other people - the more you describe your vision from a place of certainty and clarity, the more other people will understand how they can support and help you.

Gaining formal support, for example from a colleague, manager, team, budget holder or funding agency. You will be expected to be able to clearly state your aims and objectives before receiving financial support or the allocation of other resources such as time and staffing. Typically the aims and objectives will be stated at the start of a presentation, written report or funding bid.

Networking situations - you may only have a brief few minutes to communicate your message when you meet somebody new. Very often people who can support and help us pop up at the most unexpected moments and as a result of a passing comment we suddenly find there is a common connection.

Activity 1 – Aims and objectives

Aims - Firstly write your goal statement in the space below.

I want…

_____

_____

_____

_____

_____

Objectives - Write at least three (and no more than five) clear and precise steps that you will take in order to achieve what you want in the box overleaf.

1 _____

_____

2 _____

_____

3 _____

_____

4 _____

_____

5 _____

_____

Action planning and a personal development plan

Now that you have clear aims and objectives, it's time to formulate your next steps in a way that is tangible. You will be able to move forward against a timetable. An action plan and a personal development plan (PDP) will enable you to do this and you can hold yourself accountable for whether or not you make things happen by setting clear steps and deadlines.

An **action plan** will give you the steps and actions (your 'to do' list) that you need in order to turn your vision into a reality. An action plan will give you a structure for tasks and deadlines that you will undertake to meet on time. It will provide a structure for monitoring progress and make sure that you have covered everything.

A **personal development plan** will give you the opportunity to consider how you want to enhance (or add to) your personal skills and attributes in order to help implement your action plan and achieve your vision.

An action plan and personal development plan are designed to be working documents and therefore they should be updated at very regular intervals. A bit like a 'to do' list, you will be able to cross some activities off when they are completed and add new steps and actions in their place when it's appropriate to do so. Your action plans and PDP will support you best if you put all of the following in place:

- Regular review dates written in your diary.

- Regular re-drafting of your action plan to reflect your progress. Remove things you have achieved, adjust dates according to your changing circumstances and add new actions and steps as appropriate.

- Someone to whom you will be accountable – ask a colleague, friend or coach to support you, they can put your review dates in their diary with a commitment to remind you and then discuss progress with you at each agreed review stage.

The next few pages will take you through creating an action plan and personal development plan in easy steps.

Action Planning

To give your vision the steps it needs to succeed, you first need to gather together the ideas that you have generated. What could you do and what are the different you could practically take? What do you need or want to do? Write your initial ideas for your 'to do' list in the space on the next page. At this stage, there is no need to prioritise your ideas. The previous chapter will have supported you in generating some initial ideas and you can add to your 'to do' list as new steps and tasks come to mind and often as you like.

'To do' list

Activity 2 – 'To do' list

Take a look at your list and start to make notes and scribbles about the order in which you could (or should) do things. This might be dependent upon the availability of time, money or other people, as well as your own preference.

Start to prioritise the most important tasks and eliminate duplication or unnecessary steps. When you have some thoughts and notes about this, you are ready to complete a more formal action plan.

A written action plan is a more structured version of a 'to do' list. It is a tool that can support you in achieving what you want in many different areas of your life. Your vision will be broken down into smaller manageable chunks that will keep you moving forward with practical tasks. You are more likely to reach your goals within your specified timescale (or earlier) and within your budget and available resources.

There are many different ways for structuring an action plan and you may already have an action planning tool that you prefer. The beauty of using an electronic template is that you can edit and update it as many times as you like and simply print out fresh copies. Some people like to keep the 'ticked off' actions in place to show progress and provide the motivation to keep moving forward, whilst others remove actions that have been achieved and only display current and outstanding tasks. Using coloured text or highlighting whole sections in colour is a good way of giving a quick visual representation of:

- What has been completed.

- What is still outstanding.

- Where there are warning signs that deadlines are going to be missed.

- Where other problems are cropping up.

It is essential that your action plan is a working document. The worst thing that can happen is that you write it and then shut it away in a file or drawer whilst you bumble forward into the future. Instead of relying on luck, chance or fate, choose to focus, action and deliberate decisions. Your action plan will be your blueprint for getting things done. A good action plan will have four clear elements:

- The specific task.

- Who is going to do it.

- The other resources you need to complete the task.

- The timescale/deadline.

Now you are ready to put some time aside and plan the action you are going to take. You can use the template provided for you on the next page. Alternatively, design and create your own template. Keep your diary close at hand as you are likely to need it in order to complete your action plan effectively. Below is a brief explanation of the headings to guide you.

Task - This is the action or the step broken down into its simplest form. Describe in a few words something you need or want to do.

Cost - This is the monetary cost of the task. Your notes in this box should be as accurate as possible. Estimates might be the best you can do, although if it is possible to get quotes or work out the actual cost, that will be time well spent.

People - Who, specifically, do you need to help you? Is there a team of people that you need to engage with? Use their names if you know precisely who they are, otherwise a job title or description of the expertise that you need will suffice.

Communication - What methods do you need to use in order to be in touch with people? For example, will you use a mixture of email, meetings, conference calls, phone call and text, or just one or two of these? Consider which communication method is most appropriate. Emailing someone might not be as motivational as offering to buy them lunch so that you can tell them about your plans in person.

Resources - Think about how much time you need, as this tends to be the biggest resource you will require. Where are you going to make time in your diary? How much time and how often? Also consider things like transport, stationery, IT, security and the internet.

Risks - Consider what could go wrong and make a note of alternative strategies or how you might mitigate the risk.

Target date - Write down your specific deadline for each task.

> '*Our goals can only be reached through a vehicle of a plan, in which we must fervently believe and upon which we must vigorously act. There is no other route to success.*' Stephen A. Brennan

Activity 3 – Action Plan Template

Task	Cost	People Who?	Communication Who needs to know what?	Other resources needed	Possible risks What could go wrong?	Deadline Target date for completion

Display your action plan somewhere prominent (e.g. on a notice board, cupboard door, the front of your diary) so that you can continually refer to it and check your deadlines. Set yourself a routine of checking it regularly as this will ensure you are monitoring not just your progress, but also whether or not deadlines are being met by other people who are involved. An action plan may at first seem rather formal, although having one really will make a difference, so persevere. If you use an electronic calendar on your phone or computer, enter your deadlines with reminders and alarms as these will nudge you just when you need it.

Give your action plan to another person and ask them to check in with you as deadlines approach. They can hold you to account over your progress. If you are involving several people in achieving your goal, give them all a copy of your action plan so roles and responsibilities are clear. Everyone needs to know where they fit in and where they could partner (or be in touch) with others.

Set yourself (and others) some rewards and incentives for achieving key deadlines. Celebration of what has been completed will help to maintain excitement and interest and will provide a proverbial pat on the back for your efforts.

SWOT Analysis and Personal Development Plan

A personal development plan is similar to an action plan in its structure, although the focus is very different. A personal development plan will help you to reflect upon your own performance in relation to achieving your vision and then put in place learning opportunities so that you have the best skills and attributes to create and realise what you want. What skills and knowledge do you want to develop? What plan can you put in place to ensure this happens?

A SWOT analysis is a great structure to support you in answering these two questions. **SWOT** is an acronym for **Strengths, Weaknesses, Opportunities, and Threats**. The SWOT analysis model came from the research conducted at Stanford Research Institute in the 1960s and it was first described in detail by Edmund P. Learned et al, in 'Business

Policy, Text and Cases' (1969). SWOT stemmed from the need to find out why corporate planning sometimes failed. The research was to find out what could be done about such failure. The original research team (funded by the Fortune 500 companies) interviewed 5,000 managers at 1,000 companies over nine years using these categories:

- Good in the present is **S**atisfactory

- Good in the future is an **O**pportunity

- Bad in the present is a **F**ault

- Bad in the future is a **T**hreat.

This was called a **SOFT** analysis. At a seminar in Zurich in 1964, Urick and Orr changed the F to a W, and it has stuck as that; **soFt** to **sWot**.

Strengths	Weaknesses
Things about me that are good now. Maintain and build on them. I am... I can...	What is it about my skills, knowledge or behaviours that lets me down? Remedy, change or stop them.
Opportunities	**Threats**
Things that are good for the future. Prioritise them, capture them, build on them and optimise.	Things that are bad for the future. Put in plans to manage them or counter them.

Figure 20: SWOT Analysis

When you have thought out your personal development needs clearly, complete you personal development plan to ensure these needs are met.

On its own, a **SWOT analysis** can be meaningless. It works best when part of an overall strategy. Your aim is to be at your best so that you can achieve your vision. You will use a SWOT template (Activity 4) to assess your personal strengths, weaknesses plus any opportunities and threats, as you work towards your vision. In Activity 5 you apply what you learn from this process and identify new experiences and learning opportunities that you need. Then all you have to do is make it happen! An example of a completed SWOT analysis is shown below.

Strengths	Weaknesses
I am positive and focussed	I put overwhelming pressure on myself to achieve a high standard
I can communicate effectively at different levels of authority/ management	My positivity towards challenges can grate on others
I understand the structure of my organisation and its fundamental ethos	
I already have qualifications that will support me	
Opportunities	**Threats**
Exciting opportunities with new job structures being created	Other personal commitments Time constraints within my job
Funding has been set aside to assist with staff training	

Figure 21: SWOT Analysis – Terry's example

Simple rules for a successful SWOT analysis

- Be realistic about your strengths and weaknesses.

- Distinguish between where you are today, and where you could be in the future.

- Be specific and avoid grey areas.

- Always analyse in relation to your competition i.e. I am better than or worse than ...

- Keep your SWOT short, simple and 'fit for purpose'.

- Avoid unnecessary complexity and over analysis.

Activity 4 – Your personal SWOT analysis

In a copy of the SWOT grid (see the next page), make notes about your perceptions in the following areas:

- Your strengths and weaknesses in achieving your vision.

- Your strengths and weaknesses as a learner.

- The opportunities and threats (for your learning and development) that might be ahead of you as you work towards achieving your goal.

It might help to re-state your goal before you begin.

I want...

_____

_____

_____

Strengths	Weaknesses
Things about me that are good now. Maintain and build on them. I am... I can...	What is it about my skills, knowledge or behaviours that lets me down? Remedy, change or stop them.

Opportunities	Threats
Things that are good for the future. Prioritise them, capture them, build on them and optimise.	Things that are bad for the future. Put in plans to manage them or counter them.

Now you've completed the SWOT analysis above, you will have a clearer idea of your strengths and your best attributes. In order to be at your most effective, what could you learn or develop? This could be new skills, knowledge or personal qualities. There are many different types of training or personal development activities that you could seek.

Now you can start to create your personal development plan (PDP). The process is very similar to action planning, except the focus is on your learning and development. Personal development plans (sometimes called personal development reviews) are used extensively in the workplace, often as an integrated part of a performance management or appraisal system.

Before you complete your PDP, ask yourself the following questions:

- What do I need to work on most?
- How do I prefer to study?
- What is my motive for learning?
- What qualifications and/or experience do I already have?
- What method of learning would suit me best?
- How much time do I have to complete my learning?
- What effect will learning have on different aspects of my life?
- Are there any imminent changes to my lifestyle?
- What is my ultimate goal for my learning and development?
- How will I measure my success?
- Where can I get help and advice?

Once you have considered all of the factors, you can decide on your future learning adventure. This may be one single learning goal, or many smaller steps that make up the final learning and development solution. The question of how to get there can be answered by splitting your learning task into bite-size pieces in a PDP. Just like an action plan, this is a good way to plan effectively without losing sight of your overall aim.

Complete the template on the next page.

Activity 5 – Personal Development Plan

WHAT?	WHY?	HOW?	WHEN?	RESOURCES?	MEASURES?
What skills and /or knowledge and/or behaviours do I need to develop	What specific objectives/ requirements will this development help me to achieve in relation to my goal?	What specific development activities will I undertake?	Target or review date	What is needed to make this happen? (e.g. time, support, finance)	How will I know when I have achieved this?

'The secret of getting ahead is getting started. The secret of getting started is breaking your complex overwhelming tasks into small manageable tasks, and then starting on the first one.'

Mark Twain

Chapter TEN

VISION
S is for Start

'Just because we know the best way froward doesn't mean we will actually take it.'

Paul McGee

VISIONS – S is for Start

The title of this book is VISION and I have added a seventh stage to the VISION system. There are a few reasons for this.

Firstly, I didn't want to call the book VISIONS as I thought it might suggest something a bit weird that is induced after too much alcohol or drugs!

Secondly, there is a commonly held view that the brain chunks information best in odd numbers (groups of three, five, seven or nine bits of information). George Miller wrote (1956) argues that the number of objects an average human can consciously hold is 7 ± 2 (between 5 and 9 things). This is a commonly accepted principle for accelerating learning and for helping information presented to be more memorable and retainable.

Thirdly and most importantly in my view, if there is no action, the vision will remain a vision and you will never know if it could have been made a wonderful reality. Therefore a 7th stage was needed and S stands for Start.

S could also stand for steps. Think about literally taking steps - go out for a walk, a run or some other physical activity. This will clear your head and you will probably find that you talk to yourself about your vision in your head. This helps to think things through. You might go into a trance-like state where your mind just wanders and you become less aware of your surroundings. New ideas and insights may come to mind. Successful visionary people take part in physical activity and in addition to the health benefits of relaxation and exercise, they say how it also helps them to think or make decisions.

Taking part in a physical activity alone and outdoors is most effective. This is because there are less external distractions (such as another person chatting to you or a TV screen) and it enables you to be firmly back in first position (see chapter five) where you are thinking about your goals and ambitions as yourself; a place where decisions and actions are simpler and more motivational for you.

So the message is **Start** - do **Something** and take some **Steps**.

It is now your responsibility to make something happen. It doesn't matter how big or small your first step. What is important here is taking some sort of action to get the momentum going. In the last chapter you created the first draft of your action plan and personal development plan, so this will provide you with some possible first steps. An action plan is a great thing to have and maybe you have proudly stuck it on a wall or in a folder. However, unless you do something, it will have been a waste of time and energy. That's not what you want, is it?

3 PART THREE

'Some people dream of success, whilst others wake up and work hard at it.'

Unknown

Chapter ELEVEN

VISION
How do you
measure up?

'Vision without action is merely a dream.
Action without vision just passes the time.
Vision with action can change the world.'

Joel A Barker

VISION – How do you measure up?

Now that you have worked with the VISION system, you are well on your way to becoming truly visionary! Do you think you are nearly there or is there still a long way to go? Somewhere in between perhaps?

In chapter three, you scored your starting point with each element of the VISION system from 1 to 10. You may have produced a visual score similar to the picture below or maybe you wrote your scores down somewhere else.

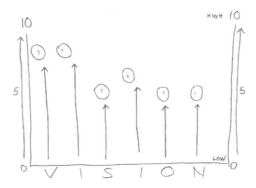

Figure 22: VISION self assessment from chapter three

Activity 1

The first step in measuring yourself against the base line scores from chapter 3 is to create a new set of scores. Decide how well you are now performing in each of the seven steps and give yourself a mark out of 10 for each step. Make a note of your scores on the next page.

	V	I	S	I	O	N	S
Score							

The highest scores would mean that having experienced each step of VISION, you feel you are already extremely good at this aspect of the system. A low score would mean that you still know very little or have few skills in this area. Go with your instinct and score in the way that feels right for you.

Activity 2

Firstly, go back to chapter three and look at your base line scores for VISION. Write them in the first column provided below.

Secondly, take your new scores (your new level of understanding, skills and success) and enter these scores in the second column. Add some notes in the comments box. There are two completed examples to guide you on the next page.

	Score before using VISION	Score after using VISION	Comments
V			
I			
S			
I			
O			
N			
S			

Example 1 – Case study – Sally

	Score before using VISION	Score after using VISION	Comments
V	5	7	Further work on Values is the area that will help me most because it's the first step. When I get this right the next steps in the VISION system will fall into place and they will all work better for me. I am definitely going to start to action this right away.
I	4	8	
S	4	8	
I	7	9	
O	6	7	
N	2	8	
S	8	10	

Example 2 – Case study – Terry

	Score before using VISION	Score after using VISION	Comments
V	7	9	I want to go back and spend more time on the images, inspiration and ideas. I want to further develop visuals for my goal and use more vision boards. This will link into providing more creative options and opportunities for me. My biggest challenge is getting started. I have a habit of saying I will do things and then I don't. I am going to ask a friend to check up on my deadlines.
I	8	9	
S	6	8	
I	3	5	
O	5	7	
N	5	6	
S	5	6	

Now give yourself a pat on the back for all your hard work and notice the difference this has made to your scores. The last part of this activity is to reflect on what further work would be useful at this stage (if any).

Which part of the VISION system would it most useful to go back to and why?

What benefits will you gain from doing further work in this area of VISION?

Just like Sally and Terry on the previous page, I am sure you now have an improved VISION of the future you want.

Some days you will waiver and be enveloped by day to day tasks flowing constantly around you. You will face problems, obstacles and disappointments.

Other days you will surface above the constantly moving stream of events and take a moment to check out where you want to be and the progress you are making. Your Action Plan has provided the starting point, with a structure and timescales for you to do this. The final two chapters will provide some guidance on how to keep going. Ultimately, it's down to you!

> *'I have missed more than 9000 shots in my career. I have lost almost 300 games. 26 times I have been trusted to take the game winning shot and missed. I've failed over and over and over again in my life. And that is why I succeed.'* Michael Jordan

Chapter TWELVE

Peripheral VISION

'Every man takes the limits of his own field of vision for the limits of the world.'

Arthur Schopenhauer

Peripheral VISION

Much of what we are taught about achieving our goals suggests that a determined focus on the goal is essential. I don't disagree with this, although my suggestion is that from time to time, you should lose your direct focus on your goal, widen your peripheral vision and notice what appears. This chapter will explain how to do this and why it could help you be more effective in achieving what you want.

The best way to describe how peripheral vision works is to imagine a time in the past when you were learning to drive a car. What you were concentrating on as you were being taught? Then notice where your focus is now that you have been driving for some time. Activity 1 will take you through this exercise in more detail.

Activity 1 – The experience of learning to drive

Step 1 - Imagine sitting in the car during your first few driving lessons. You are holding the wheel and looking through the windscreen. Write down some words that describe how you felt. What were you noticing through the windscreen? What were you seeing? What were you hearing?

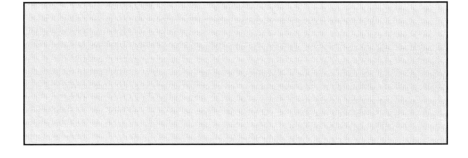

I expect some of your words capture feelings such as stress and anxiety. Your focus through the windscreen is probably on the road and car immediately in front of you. My daughters have both learnt to drive recently and I can still remember their deep concentration and heightened alertness of every gear change and manoeuvre as they paid conscious attention to doing several new things at once.

Step 2 - Now imagine sitting in the car as if it is today and notice your different posture and feelings. Look through the windscreen and write down what you notice on your journey as you drive along. Maybe you have driven in the last day or so and you can write down what you saw, heard and felt.

Now compare these words with Step 1. What do you notice? On my journey into town recently I saw three roe deer on the hill to the left of me and a buzzard circling above a group of oak trees. Would I have noticed these as a learner driver? Probably not. My focus would have been directly ahead and within a short distance of the car.

Peripheral vision is the area of vision just outside your line of sight or side vision (Collins Dictionary 2013). When you utilise peripheral vision, you can concentrate on the road ahead and also notice and pay attention to other things too. Your sub-conscious takes care of many of the mechanics of moving forward. As an experienced driver you are competent at some of the skills needed and you don't need to consciously employ them. Now that you have been driving for a long time, do you consciously think and plan every gear change and movement of the indicator or do some of your driving skills operate seamlessly and gracefully? How often do you arrive at a destination with little awareness of how you got there?

Peripheral vision puts us in a state of parasympathetic nervous arousal (PNA). This is normally a healthy state of comfort and relaxation where the body rests, digests and restores itself. Heart rate, blood pressure and temperature all drop, endorphins are released and processing of thoughts and levels of creativity increase. Interestingly, if the PNA state is too deep or prolonged, it can lead to a freeze state such as numbness, clouded thinking, chronic fatigue and even depression (V. Mead 2012).

The opposite of this is the adrenalin driven sympathetic nervous arousal (SNA) which stimulates and stresses us. It is responsible for flight or fight responses. The narrower focus of foveal vision (tunnel vision at its extreme) is there to potentially save your life, a principle which learner drivers can probably identify with! It reduces spontaneity; and your memories, skills and learning are less accessible to you.

Have you ever been in a situation where you want to recall an immediate fact from the depths of your memory and the more you think about it, the less you can get hold of it? As soon as you've walked away from the situation where you were focussing on it, it pops into mind. Very frustrating. This illustrates the impact of the sympathetic nervous state (SNA) compared to the parasympathetic state (PNA). A healthy nervous system maintains balances input between PNA and SNA within a normal day.

Peripheral vision creates a state of relaxed alertness and amongst other things, it is used for speed reading and as a stress management technique. It creates different neural pathways in the brain and takes in more of what is happening around us. When we were hunter-gatherers it allowed us to see our prey and track their movements without giving ourselves away and if you are a teacher, it gives you the very useful gift of being able to talk to one person in the room and still notice what the rest of the class are up to!

Peripheral vision will help you to disperse your fears about what you want to achieve and it will let new things into your awareness that maybe you've not thought of before.

> *'Recently, I was planning a talk to give to a networking group and I found myself getting bogged down in the detail and timings of how I was going to structure the session. I wasn't making any progress so I decided to take a break and headed out for a run for an hour. Whilst I was running across an open countryside track I found myself drifting into a relaxed place in my mind. A place where not a lot happens and thoughts come and go. All of a sudden, a brand new idea came to mind, combining a couple of workshop activities I'd not given a second thought to for months. Frustratingly, I didn't have anything with me to write this new idea down and I spent the last section of my run doing my best to consciously hold onto it until I got back to my desk.'*
>
> – Richard

Richard's story shows the power of the parasympathetic state that peripheral vision can create. TV and computers have the opposite effect to this. They keep you in focussed (foveal) vision more and more in your daily life. Reducing the time you spend in peripheral vision limits your ability to noticing new things, learn and be creative.

If you are too focussed on your goal, you might lose sight of what is going on around you and opportunities that might present themselves. It is sometimes good to take away your strong focus on your goal or ambition and relax. Continue to think about it in the 'now' (a state of day dreaming or even trance) and notice your new thoughts.

Go outdoors and be active

Visionary people will tell you about the importance of outdoor physical activity in shaping and deepening their vision and giving them the confidence to take action.

Physical activity should be outside wherever possible as the spaces are larger and more open. The nature of the activity can vary hugely (hill walking, mountain biking, sailing, road cycling, strolling round the park to walk the dog or taking a break at lunch to walk in the grounds at work). The effect of this is the same in all cases – it creates peripheral vision and a state of relaxation. This in turn will heighten your instinctive abilities and create states of alertness, relaxation, openness and happiness.

Next time you want to deliberately consider taking steps towards your goal (s), go for a walk and notice what happens. Any open space will do and the more open it is, the better. Head for a wide boulevard, city park, sports fields or some open countryside. It's not contact with nature that is the key, so don't be put off if your open space is an urbanscape as that won't matter at all. Avoid narrow streets with tall buildings or areas with lots of trees as they will increase your focus. The wider the view, the better.

Resist the temptation to plug into an MP3 player and gaze at your feet as both of these encourage focus rather than wider vision. As long as it is safe to do so, lift your gaze in to the distance ahead and allow your mind to be still.

If access to movement outdoors is limited for you, choose your space indoors carefully. Sitting on the sofa is better for peripheral vision than being at a desk. There might be a big window out onto a garden, car park or city rooftop view and this is better for peripheral vision than looking at a partition, wall or notice boards. Your creativity and concentration on a big task should improve with the additional visual space.

Here is another way to overcome limited time or opportunity for physical activity outdoors. By practising this next exercise you can still think about your goal in a state of peripheral vision:

- Choose a spot on a wall that is straight in front of you (the distance away doesn't matter) and slightly above eye level.

- Look at that point in a concentrated way for a short while and notice as the room around you starts to become fuzzy.

- Carry on looking at the point and start to pay attention to what is either side of that point. Notice what you can see out of the corner of your eyes. You will start to relax and many people notice their hands get warmer (this is because parasympathetic nervous arousal increases blood flow to the extremities of your body as your heart rate slows and less blood is needed by your vital organs).

- Now think about your goal whilst holding this relaxed gaze and see what new insights come to mind.

Narrow vision can hamper your learning and ability to make connections between different experiences and new opportunities. Devotion to your goals and deep focus on achieving them might actually be counter-productive. Develop your peripheral vision, get active outdoors, find wider landscapes and discover how a wider field of vision will develop your intuition and learning.

Finally, let me take you back to chapter one and the way we looked at the difference between having a goal and having a vision. You will remember that Michael Neill suggests spending less time concentrating on goals and more time on 'good work'. This supports the notion of engaging peripheral vision rather than foveal vision by being 'in the now' more often and focussed into the future less often. By noticing more of what is around you in the moment, you may gain more opportunities and attract more of what you want compared to directing our attention almost exclusively into the future. A balance of both is healthy, not just for your goals but also for your mind and body too.

> *'Establishing goals is all right if you don't let them deprive you of interesting detours.'* Doug Larson

Chapter THIRTEEN

Super
VISION

'The difference between ordinary and extraordinary is that little extra.'

Jimmy Johnson

Super VISION

How about some supervision?

How can you also supervise yourself?

Here is a great tool based on John McWhirter's hierarchical model of Performance, Management and Direction. This model will help you to find any potential sources of weakness in your actions and performance, taking it forward. You can be your own best supervisor over the coming weeks, months or years.

As with many of the activities in this book, this exercise can be done in several ways:

- Sit down on your own with a piece of paper, a pen and quiet thinking time.

- Sit down with a coach who can take you through the process and push you a little more out of your comfort zone than you might otherwise experience whilst coaching yourself.

- Stand up and use different spaces on the floor to create a spatial sorting exercise – lay out floor cards and walk between the four areas shown on the next page (with or without a coach to guide you).

Activity 1 – Super-VISION

Step 1 - Take five pieces of paper and create five place mats for the floor as shown by the diagram below.

Step 2 - Remind yourself of your current level of performance in achieving your vision – refer back to your scores in chapter eleven.

Step 3 - Take an aspect of your goal or the VISION system and ask yourself 'What score do I want to achieve out of 10 in this area of my goal?' Hold that thought and step into the context space.

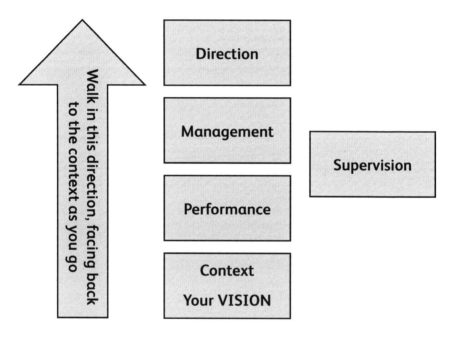

Figure 23: The super-VISION activity (after McWhirter)

Step 4 - Performance – Step into this space and turn back to face the context.

- What are you doing?

- What aren't you doing?

- What is important here?

Step 5 - Management – Step into this space facing performance and context.

- How do you know what to do and when?

- How do you know which options to choose?

- How are you collecting and evaluating feedback?

Step 6 - Direction – Step into this space facing Management, Performance and Context.

- Why do you choose to do these things?

- Why did you arrive at this thinking?

- Why is all of this important?

Step 7 - Supervision – Step into this space so that you can notice everything else – look across and consider these questions:

- What are you noticing?

- What suggestions do you need to make?

- What additional awareness is required?

Step 8 - Take all the suggestions coming from supervision and work your way back down the floor cards – start in Direction, move to Management, return to Performance and as you go, make adjustments to your thinking as you see fit.

Step 9 - Move into context – your VISION – what is your level of performance now from 1-10?

As a result of this activity, what are you going to stop doing?

_____

_____

_____

_____

_____

_____

Start doing?

_____

_____

_____

_____

_____

_____

Conclusion

The idea for this book came from my own personal lack of understanding of vision. It is a word that I have heard used frequently and causally over the years, especially in the workplace. I'd never really understood what it meant, although it was clearly felt to be of major importance to have 'vision' or be a 'visionary'.

What I have aimed to do with the book is firstly give clarity about what vision means and how it differs from having a goal. Goals are a good thing. Vision is something very special. I wanted you to understand how they are different and share that difference with you.

Step 1 - Values - in this first stage, you uncovered the important thing(s) about your vision for the future.

Step 2 - Identity - knowing who you are in relation to your vision is very powerful. You have been thinking about the identities which are going to be helpful and resourceful in achieving what you want.

Step 3 - Stories - you are developing compelling evidence for your vision. The DESERT and PEOPLE story-telling systems are helping you achieve this.

Step 4 - Images - you have spent time creating images of your future and the steps for getting there, in a way that not only supports you personally, but can also be described or shown to others.

Step 5 - Options - there are a number of options available to you. The more options you have, the more flexibility you can exhibit when working with others and overcoming challenges.

Step 6 - Next steps - action planning and personal development planning has provided structure and timescales for your future actions.

Step 7 - Start!

Enjoy VISIONeering and make the difference that you know you can.

Shelf development or self development?

5 things to do before you put this book back on a shelf:

1 _____

_____

2 _____

_____

3 _____

_____

4 _____

_____

5 _____

_____

References

Adams, R. L. (2013). *How not to give up: a motivational and inspirational guide to goal setting and achieving your dreams.* Amazon Media EU S.à r.l.

Bateson, M. (1994). *Peripheral Visions.* Harper Collins Publishers, New York.

Bostic St Clair, C. & Grinder, J. (2001). *Whispering in the Wind.* J&C Enterprises, Scotts Valley, California.

Bandler, R. & Grinder, J. (1981). *Frogs into Princes.* Real People Press, Lafayette, California.

Bridges, W. & Mitchell, S. (2000). *Leading Transition: A New Model for Change.* Leader to Leader. 16 (Spring 2000): 30-36.

Buzan, T. (1974). *Mind Mapping, Use Your Head.* BBC Books, London.

Carroll, Lewis. (1865). *Alice's Adventures in Wonderland.*

Collingwood, C. & Thompson, R. *Mirror Neurons: The Neuropsychology of NLP Modeling.* Available at http://www.inspiritive.com.au/nlp-research/modelling-mirror-neurons.htm

Covey, S. (1989). *The Seven Habits of Highly Effective People.* Free Press, New York.

Collins English Dictionary 2013. Available at www.collinsdictionary.com

DeLozier, J. and Grinder, J. (1987). *Turtles All the Way Down.* Metamorphous Press, Portland.

Dilts, R. (1990). *Changing Belief Systems with NLP.* Meta-Publications, Capitola, CA.

Debra Jinks and Dexter, J. and Jinks, D.(2012): *What do you Really Want: An Examination of the Pursuit of Goal Setting in Coaching.* International Journal of Evidence Based Coaching and Mentoring, Vol 10, No 2 pp. 100 – 110.

Gallese, V., Fadiga, L., Fogassi, L. & Rizzolatti, G. (1996). *Action recognition in the premotor cortex*. Brain, 119,593-609.

Gorski, Roger. Professor of Neurobiology, University of California, Los Angeles. http://people.healthsciences.ucla.edu/research/institution/personnel?personnel_id=45954

Hill, N. (1928). *The Law of Success in Sixteen Lesson*s. Tribeca Books, US.

Hill, N. (1937). *Think and Grow Ric*h. The Ralston Society, US.

Ishikawa, Kaoru. (1968). *Guide to Quality Control* (Japanese): JUSE Press, Ltd, Gemba No QC Shuho, Tokyo.

Kotter, J. (1996). *Leading Change*. Harvard Business Review Press, US.

Edmund P. Learned, C. Roland Christiansen, Kenneth Andrews, and William D. Guth. (1969). *Business Policy, Text and Cases*. R. D. Irwin, US.

Loo, T. *How to use a vision board to activate the law of attraction*. Available at www.selfgrowth.com/articles/How_to_Use_a_Vision_Board_to_Activate_the_Law_of_Attraction

McGee, P. (2005). *S.U.M.O*. Capstone Publishing Ltd, Chichester.

McWhirter, J. (2012). *Course Manual: DBM(R) Masters, University of Valencia, Spain*. www.sensorysytems.co.uk

Mead, V. www.veroniquemead.com/ pns.php

Miller, G. A. (1956). *The Magical Number Seven plus or minus two: Some limits on our capacity for processing information*. Psychological Review, 63, 81-97.

Neill, M. (2013). *The Inside Out Revolution*. Hay House, UK.

Pease, A. & B. (1999). *Why men don't listen and women can't read map*s. Orion, London.

Schwarz, J. (2008). *The Vision Board: The secret to an extraordinary life*. Harper Collins, New York.

Valeti, M. (2011) – *Short Stories with Moral* http://www.scribd.com/doc/53335861/62/The-Arrogant-Swans

Wattles, W. (1910). *The Science of Getting Rich*. Elizabeth Towne Company, Holyoke, Massachusetts.

Wiseman, R. (2007). www.quirkology.com/UK/Experiment_ resolution

Whitmore, J. (2002). *Coaching for Performance*. Nicholas Brealey Publishing Ltd, London.

Wikihow. www.wikihow.com/Be-Charismatic

Inspirational quotes – who are they?

James Allen (1864 - 1912) – writer.

Joel A Barker – author, and speaker.

William Blake (1757 - 1827) – poet.

Stephen A Brennan – basketball coach.

Jim Collins – business consultant, author and lecturer.

Walt Disney (1901 - 1966) – film producer and entrepreneur.

Albert Einstein (1879 - 1955) – physicist.

Henry Ford (1863 - 1947) – industrialist.

Tony Gaskins – author and speaker.

Shakti Gawain – author.

Harold Clarke Goddard (1878 - 1950) – professor.

L. Michael Hall – entrepreneur and author.

Bill Harris – coach, author and entrepreneur.

Napoleon Hill (1883 -1970) – author.

Hilary Hinton "Zig" Ziglar (1926 - 2012) – author, salesman, and speaker.

Tom Hooper – film and television director.

Janet Jackson – recording artist and actress.

Jimmy Johnson – former American football player, coach and now a broadcaster.

Michael Jordan – former professional basketball player.

Carl Jung (1875 - 1961) – psychotherapist and psychiatrist.

Doug Larson – newspaper columnist.

Janet Litherland – author.

David Lloyd George (1863 - 1945) – politician and statesman.

Paul McGee – the Sumo Guy and professional speaker.

Michael Neill – author, radio host and life coach.

Kevin O'Rourke – songwriter.

Joy Page (1924 - 2008) – actress.

Bob Proctor – author, coach and entrepreneur.

Jim Rohn (1930 - 2009) – author, speaker and entrepreneur.

Arthur Schopenhauer (1788 - 1860) – philosopher.

Jimmy Sweeney – career coach and author.

Brian Tracy – speaker, author and life coach.

Mark Twain (1835 - 1910) – author.

Afterword

VISION – The beginnings

I hope you've enjoyed working with this book and feel excited and energised about the future that awaits you.

Have you ever had the feeling when an idea just won't go away? It's there in the back of your mind all the time and every now and again it pops up and gives you a kick and says, 'I'm still here, what are you going to do about it?'.

That is exactly what happened to me when I had the idea for this book, although I knew I hadn't yet arrived at a brilliant enough structure to make it work. I expect you've had situations in the past where the harder you think the less the answer comes. The idea finally came to me in the spring of 2012 when I least expected it. I was driving over the Wiltshire Downs on the A361 to Devizes, on my way back from a meeting in Swindon. I love this stretch of road and it was my Mum's favourite journey in the whole of Britain! The landscapes are wide and rolling and the colours are soft tones of greens and browns. In spring the fields are yellow when the oilseed rape is in flower.

As I was driving along, keeping my eyes out for hares and deer in the distance, it popped from my unconscious to consciousness – the final idea for VISION – a tah da! moment. In chapter twelve I write about the power of the relaxed state of peripheral vision for learning and creativity, which I think is exactly what had happened to me on this particular day. I pulled over in the bus stop at the superstore on the edge of Devizes and wrote the acronym VISION down quickly on a scrap of paper. The book was born!

Want to know more?

Why not invite Clare Smale as a speaker for your next conference or event?

Email: clare@inspired2learn.co.uk

www.inspired2learn.co.uk

www.transformyourgoalswithvision.com

Additional resources

Visit the website for this book where you will be able to download templates for the activities in VISION, plus bonus materials. Now that you have experienced the book, you might like to join an event or course. Develop your skills with direct support from Clare and her team. Events are published on the website and through social media.

Please get in touch with your success stories and feedback so that we can make the VISION system even better in the future.

VISION for your organisation

Clare Smale runs workshops and training events and speaks at conferences. VISION can be tailored to suit your needs and adapted for working with teams, coaches or leaders at all levels. You can book Clare to deliver the principles of this book for your organisation. Your workshop or training will be interactive and engaging and will include resources and materials for you to keep.

 VISION courses are formally recognised and certificated by the Institute of Leadership and Management (ILM) as Development Programmes.

VISION for Schools

Clare taught in secondary schools for 13 years before establishing a successful business training and developing others. She has continued to work extensively in schools and with teachers. Here is a selection of what she can offer for your school through workshops, INSET days, coaching, conferences or facilitation:

- Coaching and mentoring skills: training and accreditation.

- Personal coaching at all levels.

- Leadership & management development.

- Speaking at conferences and events.

- Interpersonal skills and personal development events.

About the author

Clare Smale is a highly respected coach, trainer and speaker.

Clare has over 20 years experience of supporting people to be at their best. Before founding inspired2learn with her husband in 2002, she was a teacher and leader in three 11-18 comprehensive schools and she has spent the last eleven years as a trainer and performance coach for a wide variety of private and public sector organisations. Clare's particular interests are in helping leaders and managers to tackle the challenges associated with managing change and team working, with a focus on personal development and resilience.

Clare is a trained and accredited coach, NLP Master Practitioner and NLP Trainer. Over the years, she has helped thousands of people achieve their goals. Her work with young people includes voluntary youth coaching for Inner Flame and the Coach in Every City project (supported by the Knowledge to Action Foundation and Youth Coaching Academy UK) and supporting young people into employment through Plan 500, a business mentoring project in Swindon.

Testimonials for VISION

'This is not just a book to read but to engage with. It's packed with insights and ideas to help you achieve and fulfil your vision. In a world of hype this book actually provides the help you require to create a compelling future.'

Paul McGee, author of SUMO and How to Stop Worrying

'There's a big difference to the simplistic approaches to goals and goal-setting that we see in so many self-help or coaching books and the simple but effective tools that can help us manage the real-life complexity of setting and managing challenging goals. Whether or not we achieve meaningful goals depends on a great many contextual factors, both within ourselves and within the systems, of which we are a part. Clare Smale achieves the difficult task of providing a simple toolkit and framework that acknowledges and works within this complexity.'

David Clutterbuck, Special Ambassador, European Mentoring and Coaching Council

'Clare has written a focussed and clear guide to identifying your vision. The simplicity of this book is its greatest attraction, because Clare acts as your guide, breaking down your journey into easily achievable and manageable steps. Commit to the VISIONS journey using this workbook as your guide, and I am confident you will transform your goals into a more meaningful and motivational vision.'

Karen Moxom, Director of the Association for NLP

'It is fantastic to see such an inspiring and rewarding book arise from the process of NLP modelling'.

Fran Burgess, author of the NLP Cookbook

'It's rare to find such a well-written, considered and practical guide to getting exactly what you want. Clare's depth of understanding of what makes outcomes really happen shines from this book. Every manager, leader, worker and home-maker would benefit from the clarity of the processes in this book. Stacked with brilliant, easy-to-follow and immediately useful tools, this is the Holy Grail of self development and leadership, in the sense that we all need to know where we are going and how we are going to get there. 'Vision' brings together the very best knowledge, understanding and techniques for self efficacy and organisational development. I highly recommend this superb addition to the personal and professional effectiveness genre.'

Will Thomas, Performance Coach, award-winning and best-selling author

'This is a deceptively powerful book; it's warm, inviting and fun to look at but actually it's a tiger in lambs clothing. Clare has effectively trawled the minds of some of our greatest thinkers and distilled their wisdom in one place, then wrapped it in a logical, practical yet encouraging structure. Anyone seriously intending to realise significant change in their circumstances would do well to work through the methods described here. With just one word of caution – be careful what you wish for!'

Julie Starr, author of The Coaching Manual and Brilliant Coaching

'Don't be afraid to take a big step if one is indicated; you can't cross a chasm in two small jumps.'

David Lloyd George